MW01702485

Stones Alive! 3

Volume 3 of the Stones Alive! Trilogy

Translating the Crystalline Grid

Marilyn & Tohmas
Twintreess

Offered to you from the hearts of the Stonebeings and

AhhhMuse

2340 US Hwy 180 E. #171

Silver City, NM 88061 USA

800-585-9389 575-534-0410

www.ahhhmuse.com www.abundanceofahhhmuse.com

Please find us anytime at ahhhmuse@juno.com

We are honored to hear from you.

First Edition.

Printed in the United States of America

ISBN# 1-890808-04-0

Cover photo: Tohmas Twintreess and Alaska Stock Images

Graphic Design: Charlotte Krebs-Holtz of Salmagundi Design

We share this information with you from our own Spirits listening to the Spirits of the Stones. We intend it as a pure gift from which you then will listen to your own Spirits and the Stones in your own perfect way.

We are not telling you to do anything from this book to heal, or to "fix" yourself; that would be disrespectful. As ever, we invite you to listen to your OWN heart, to your own doctors and to your own trusted advisers for whatever help, prescriptions, and guidance that you need. We all walk our own perfect journey.

Also, this book is copyrighted because that is how we utterly honor the Stonebeings' perfect words and ways. We do not edit them; we simply accept their messages in exactly the way that they offer them and place them in the form in which they have asked to be presented. It is part of our thanks and honoring of them to ask everyone else to respect them in this way, as well.

Other Titles by Twintreess

"Stones Alive!, Volume 2: Listening More Deeply
to the Gifts of the Earth

"Stones Alive!, Volume 1: A Reference Guide to Stones
for the New Millennium"

"Stones Alive! The Rituals of Manifestation Deck"

"House as Teacher: Building the Future Now, Creating Sacred Space in the New Millennium (by Twintreess and Ursela Gurau)

"Ogallalah de Oro: My Life with Humans"

"Etheric Songs from the Children of Earth"

"The Heart of Matter"

Upcoming Titles

"The Rituals of Manifestation Deck Workbook"

"Kahlill: Conscious Child Listening"

Table of Contents

For You

We love you!

To all the Stonebeings

who walk in these pages with almost unbearable kindness.

To the Sun Grandfather (hi hi hi!)

who beams continually creativity down upon us.

To the Earth Mother

who gives us a home where we join body and soul

ever, ever closer together.

To you,

reading this journey with us,

we give you our open heart

never consciously knowing if you clasped it to yours

or if you threw it away to do something else.

We offer this to all of you

because we can,

because it is in our cells to do this—

to share stories across Spirits.

We write this in the constantly present tense

because we did not dedicate this book,

one moment only.

We do dedicate it now

and that re-blossoms every moment

in our breath and in our hearts.

We visited this dedication continually while writing this book.

We visit again and again and again

now

to remind us why we are here.

Statement of Intent

We are here.

We are now.

We unconditionally bridge to and from the world of Stones

to and from the world of 2-leggeds

and share their stories,

with those who are truly willing.

We are utterly grateful.

This is our joy, our life.

We invite our Spirits to join us in this sacred conversation

and to join us in

Freedom

Immortality

& Invisibility.

Thanks to all always.

If You Truly Want to Listen to Stones

Before entering this book adventure any further, let's pause.

We live in a very busy world, don't we?

That usually means that we do things as quickly as we can, trying to squeeze in every thing we HAVE to do—let alone anything we want to do.

And as we do things as fast as we can, what do we get out of it?

Do we get everything done?

Nope, because there is always more work to do.

Are we satisfied that we did the best we could?

Not usually. If we're just doing things as quickly as we can, we usually don't put ourselves into them, and afterwards, we're left feeling empty, or like we just haven't done enough, or that we somehow haven't done them well. It's true: If you put yourself whole-body-and-soul into anything (ANYTHING at all), you will receive everything magnificent, wondrous and glorious, and more.

So let's pause here.

Just drop everything except reading these pages full-out,

with your heart sttreeetttchinng

just listening,

just listening.

At first, you may just hear old rumblings of grocery lists

and petulant head-voices that shout,

"It's not working! It's not working! See, I told you it wouldn't work."

Stay with it, impatience and all.

Before you can hear anything really meaningful—something so wonderful it makes you gasp—you have to give all the habitual

chitter-chatter the chance to be heard, too.

After all, these chatterings are your defenses. They protect you from everything new—whether it's ultimately good or bad for you, or not.

Defenses just point-blank shoo away the unknown....just in case...

So listen to them so that you can honor the **good** work they have done (After all you made it here today, didn't you? That counts for something.).

When you really listen, you'll be able to tell the unjustified fears, "Everything's fine. I don't want you to protect me from listening to the Stonebeings. Nothing's trying to hurt me. I WANT to do this."

Eventually, the defenses will believe you, because you actually **listened** to them—you truly considered what they were saying. Anything in you that's been honestly respected and listened to will ultimately respect the rest of you. That will give you a small breath of peace to now focus on what you truly choose, instead of just aimlessly following the distractions. So use it! Right now make a full-out, honoring choice to listen to the Stonebeings while you are here.

Stop now.

Write down a statement that will passionately support you in this choice.

Make it a short, but ridiculously wondrous statement—something that tickles you, that delights you so much that you can hardly say it.

Actually you don't have to say it out loud—just say it to all parts of yourself when you find yourself drifting in too many needless distractions, instead of giving this Stone journey your beautiful all.

It will remind you what you **want** to listen to, body and soul, so that you can really feel alive! What could be more auspicious than listening to another consciousness, full of unimaginable wisdom and gifts?

This is the moment.

You have brought it to yourself (for some good—even if as of yet unknown—reason).

Grab it!

Ride it.

Clutch your Statement of Choice in both hands.

Offer it up to every page here.

Whenever the echoes of scattering mind chatter come in, read them your Statement of Choice, with all your heart. Do it over and over until your passion wants to do this, wants to do this above all else, for this moment..........

Now you're ready to listen.

Come back to this page as often as you need to in reading this book. Choose to remember your intent to be a Listener as you ingest instead of being a decider or a controller or even a believer. A Listener is an open heart continually being activated with and through spontaneous experience with a focus on the respectful, full hearted opening of presence in the moment, in relationship, instead of goal orientation or results. The effects will come regardless, but the open heart tends to bring us the clear and conscious results that are invisible in controlling and goal oriented behaviors.

Make the invisible visible for yourself by embracing the stories of the Stonebeings here as they are speaking them, first, before deciding anything. Let this magic and mystery propel you into a world that may have a different and illogical sense of time and space but at the same time also holds the records of all time and space and so much more. The Crystalline Grid.

To truly listen with the Stonebeings means that you can hear about the Earth Mother and all the beings upon her because you can listen to the Crystalline Grid. It is the blueprint for creation and it is moving into a blueprint of co-creation.

Before we speak any further, let us again invite you to root your bodies into the fullness of the reality of what we are discovering together right now. Go and gather together the Stonebeings that most speak to you in whatever way that you can listen to, with your heart.

Put them next to you now in whatever formation encourages the full delighting force of life to land upon you now.

If you do not have Stonebeings in your life, then simply pick one or two from the willing ones in this book. Write down their names on a piece of paper. Call their essences to you with a wide open heart.

Now you are encircled with Stones and their energies. Their stories can be offered to you right now.

Sometimes to understand what is happening on the Earth Mother, you must allow yourself to find a view that is away from it so that you can see clearly across big distances and beliefs. That is why there are words here, from beings who seem to originate from elsewhere. They have visions of the Earth Mother and her children that are difficult for you to reach by yourselves.

Everything about the Earth is recorded in the Crystalline Grid, the bones of the Earth Mother. They are the perfect embodiment of strong limits and unlimited wisdom, come together and growing in new ways.

From the Crystalline Grid, the Earth is a Star that has created a home for emotions and for learning about the love within lifeforce. It has formed itself with the dominance of water and feeling that are unique in many ways and areas. She has evolved life so that it would give bodies and voices to great emotions.

All of the Stones and Plants and most of the Animals reflect this. They live and breathe in synchronization with all of life and all of its flows.

The humans are designed differently. They come to an Earth where everything matches the seasons that dance within all beings. Humans come here and they absorb all of this and they co-create or try to co-create with the generous bounty of the Earth Mother. For Ages, the humans have learned of how to create, for they are here with great stores of creativity that they love to express. They have invented many ways to use the Earth's resources, yet, they are not yet co-creating easily.

Humans are a unique species upon the Earth Mother. They take what they believe they need or what they believe they want. They do whatever they like regardless of the already existing cycles of life here. They ignore the seasons so they can light up their skies all day and all night.

They do this because it is the blueprint for humans to come here and to experience limits with their innately unlimited nature. This has always been their calling. In order to experience limits they have reached into the fullness of their Spirits and come here with such unconditional love that they take on their lives, beginning them by releasing their conscious memory of everything divine and whole. Through their birthing, they blind themselves to their true, infinite nature. They accept the amnesia that allows them to think that they are separate from all beings. Every human echoes this experience of every other human.

Then they live always reaching back to the full divinity that originally brought them to the Earth Mother. They forgot who they were and then spent lifetimes remembering a piece at a time so that they can be both limited and unlimited.

They are moving into their unlimitedness now. All of this is recorded in the Crystalline Grid. It is the Earth library who holds the name of every being who has and does live upon the Earth. Most especially, it records every step and every journey of every human.

When you feel an undeniable urge to remember, to truly be all of your lifeforce, then go to the Grid with this intent. Honor its service and ask willingly to know about all that you are. Here you can touch every hurt that has made you mortal. You can soothe every struggle and set it free. For once you choose truly to remember everything without judgment, you will be, and are, the whole human being that your divine imprint has called forth into the world. When you speak and listen with the Grid, you know all your names and all your faces. You can forgive everything. When you do, you are whole, not just in memory or theory. You become the hologram that you began and now it is a fully expanded one and it is all constantly recorded in the Crystalline Grid for accessibility.

The Crystalline Grid shows you home and from there you can travel anywhere. The Grid is available fully to every human. All willing human beings can go there and see all of themselves. Even if you have forgotten for a little while, you can remember. All of everythng is safely stored in the stories of the Crystalline Grid. Accept them.

How this Adventure Began.....

Firstly it all begins with a **"Welcome!"** We are so pleased that you have joined us here. There are times when it seemed that all of the odds were against it, and yet of course, they were not. WE, ourselves, are odd, so of course the odds could only be for us!

We are Spiritstorygivers.

That means that one day when we joined forces (Marilyn and Tohmas and the Spirit in everything), our hearts stretched wide and we heard stories. Everything was talking. That's when we realized that every BEING and every THING *do* talk. They all have their own precious energy that interacts with everything else and that makes their stories— lots and lots of stories.

We recorded them. We studied them. We put them right into our lives so that we could be the unconditional interconnectedness happening all around us (We lived and practiced them), from the Animals, the Plants, the Stones, the Elementals (the Spirits of the Elements: Fire/ Earth/Air/Water/Ethers), the Earth Mother— mostly the nature Spirits— but we opened to every story as long as it offered respect and honored us.

We listened to Stones continually just because we like them. Sometimes when you don't have a "why" for something, anything can happen, and in our life it almost always does. The Stonebeings asked us to write a new kind of reference book with them. They honored the geology and the geography that people placed upon them so that they could find them, but once people found them, the Stones wanted to talk, to have conversations with people. Then they could offer us their special energetic gifts— ones that we could truly use in these chaotic, life and death times upon our planet.

Stones opened their hearts to us, telling us all about themselves and then showing us that they could offer us transformative energies when they were joined intentionally. They specifically gave us Stonecombinations like "Bliss," "Connecting to Your Guides," and "World Peace." The giving of these generous stories became *"Stones Alive! A Reference Guide to Stones for the New Millennium."* Each word came directly from the conversation between our Spirits and the Spirits of the Stonebeings.

Every day we opened our hearts more deeply than we knew how to (but we were spontaneously supported and guided in each moment) and realized that the Stone reference guide was a trilogy. *"Stones Alive! Volume 1"* offered the heartstories of particular Stones that knew they could uniquely help humans in the biggest evolution that they had ever known, along with particular Stonecombinations when they chose to intentionally join with and work with the Stones.

"Stones Alive! 2: Listening More Deeply to the Gifts of the Earth" was exactly that—an invitation to slip beyond *"Stones Alive! Volume 1,"* where the Stones so directly provided their stories and the energy to hear them. In *"Stones Alive! 2"* you are invited to listen to the Stones for yourselves, so that you can truly **feel** them, beginning your own, unique conversation and friendship with them.

Now, welcome to *"Stones Alive! 3: Translating the Crystalline Grid!"* Here, we listen to the Stonebeings who keep opening their hearts, their gifts and their sacred wisdom to us. Truly we don't know exactly what the journey will be because this time we all will hear the Stonebeings a little differently—just as it is meant to be. In this book, the Stones want to expand our conversations to living with them, working with them, consciously co-creating a world where we evolve together with more support than we ever imagined possible, by ourselves.

Please join us.

Every word offers its fullest heart and breath and Spirit, so that we can all live a new life where we *belong* here on the Earth Mother, where we are a part of each other so utterly that separation is just an illusion, an old focus. All of the truths of all the ages have told us this, but now they are being directly spoken to us through such infinitely kind energies that we are hearing them through our own languages and ways as a translation of the Crystalline Grid.

We freely, spontaneously, joyously, share our listenings and our stories (and other peoples' stories again) with the Stonebeings in translating the Crystalline Grid.

A 2,200 pound Black Lingam space holder of the Grid in Sedona, AZ.

From the Grandfather Black Lingam

Please join me.

Settle into yourself easily.

Let your bones unclench, so that your body will grow straighter

and stronger.

Then your being unfolds,

gently at first,

until it dances with great passion

at the thrilling of life.

Meet me there.

I am there.

I am here.

I am a 9 foot tall, 4400 pound Black Lingam that has waited until this moment of perfection to speak like this. I know these words that I offer are echoing all over the world. They pulse in your heart......and as they do that, they pulse the oceans, the mountains, they pulse endless growth and endless stillness, merged with the seasons.

From the roots of my heart, I speak with you. I speak from the core of the Crystalline Grid of the Earth Mother.

Do not try to understand that. Just let each word flawlessly land upon you like a ray of the Sun Grandfather— showing its love both visibly and invisibly. I speak from a mystery and if you respect it as one, it will teach you things that your questions don't even know to ask. There is no predictable path drawn out in a straight line before us. We have grown beyond that.

Deep within the body of the Earth, pulses the Crystalline Grid. Reach out your heart to meet it full-out and free. As you extend yourself, you remember. This grid is part of you. It forms your body as well. It gives you a place to land your destiny.

It extends out all over every part of the Earth Mother, like veins stretching out to her every limb. Like clear blood it fuels her. It revitalizes her in every season. Its currents bring her the news of every being and of every event, just as they happen. Its electricity inspires her to every awareness and empathy and she shares that unceasingly with all.

When you are born into a human body, the Crystalline Grid heralds the dawn of you! It smiles, knowing all, accepting all, even before it has begun. The imprint of the Crystalline Grid lands upon your body immediately. It gives shape to your bones and your free in-Spirited-ness, simultaneously, equally. It urges them to come together, to give you a Crystalline Grid of your own.

Touch your bones. They will tell you this ancient, perfect story. They will mirror my wordgifts. Your bones and the Earth Mother's bones— the Stones and Crystals— bestow upon us all a body to speak, to shape, to unfold, to affirm Spirit on matter— Spirit on flesh. This miracle encompasses us all.

The Crystalline Grid of the Earth Mother speaks to you, now. You hear it, because each word vibrates in your bones, echoing the truth throughout your body and being. You remember— you know— because it is time. It is your time to evolve with, and beyond, the stretch of bones and Stones, into infinity.

You know this. Just let yourself feel it, now, too. Let the electricity of the Crystalline Grid light up your currents and your heart. We are one in our feeling and in our knowing.

Guide to Reading and Feeling the Adventure!

There are two basic ways you can walk your life. One way is to measure your steps precisely so that you have plenty of energy for the whole journey, and to look out carefully in all directions so that you can see what's coming before it gets to you. That way you can grab all the lovelies that you like, and simultaneously you can stop any uglies before they land on you and end your happy journey too soon.

The other way is to LEAP off mountains before landing onto your path, so you can scare away anything that might have might have been there before you: Beyond here there be dragons! You dance with the birds and the flowers decorating the way. You see what you want to see, and make all your choices instantaneously from the pit of your never satisfied explorer's belly.

In listening with our Spiritfamilies, we have uncovered another way to walk life— Door #3, we call it. It conjures up (literally) another path— one that is born of ever brand-new and constantly freeing choices. There's no way to measure it because it is not created until the precise moment you walk it. It leaps out from your heart to join with even the tiniest, magical whispers from Life. It makes a new path. It makes new life.

With that, the new adventure begins........................

So let's be hobbits on adventure, here. (They are some of our finest friends.) By now you have astutely realized that this is NOT a book. As you open the pages, it flat-out opens its many, many hearts to you (ours, the Stones', the Crystalline Grid's, Grandfather Lingam's, etc.), landing upon yours, asking you directly, *"How will you travel your life? Safely? Boldly? Quietly? Spinningly?"*

The choices are utterly endless (just like you) and this heart-book boldly invites you to realize that "Stones Alive! 3" is actually an adventure. It is your life. It is a perfect crystallized moment that stretches out onto the road to infinity. So, Hobbits, miss nothing! This is all magic, even if some might look like dragons. JUMP into it! This is the best ride in the universe. You are an awesome, brave adventurer, and contrary to popular belief, you don't even have to do it alone. (Heroes always have help— that's how they get to be heroes.) There is always/all ways support for you. The Plants, the Animals and the Crystals share this wild ride adventure with you! It's just that humans don't usually notice them, or maybe they have been trained to think of them as lesser adventurers..... (Is it possible to be a lesser adventurer...?)

In this book-adventure, the Stones are speaking up. They will guide you along any path you choose— not just the upcoming book chapter— but any, and every, chapter of life, so why not accept the help? If you take it and it doesn't apply to you, then give thanks, get rid of it, and get some NEW help (How about Phenacite instead of Calcite, today?). Ask for whatever you need to be the brave heart that you are.

We (Marilyn and Tohmas) would like to offer some help, now. We know that for some of you, it will be a little odd to directly take in the words and the pure electricity of Stones. Of course. But just because you don't understand all of it right away doesn't mean that it's not for you- that you can't utilize the gifts of the Stones on your life adventure. Sometimes Stone listening is a learned art; human words are a learned art, too. You didn't come out of the womb, speaking English, saying, *"Hi Mom, Hi Dad! What an entry ride! Sure is nice to be here."*

So as you read the messages from the Stones that gathered together in this book-adventure just to speak with you, remember that their lifeforce is directly downloaded into the words and geometries. Those words are then lovingly placed in special categories to translate them for you, so that you will recognize exactly what Stone gifts you need to help you on your adventurer's way.

For instance, in *"Stones Alive! A Reference Guide to Stones for the New Millennium"* (Volume 1 in the "Stones Alive!" trilogy) we shared individual Stones and their gifts, from Adamite to Zoisite. Their sweet messages came in the following categories:

- **The Opening Quote** — quietly welcomes you to a new world.
- **The Physical Description** — identifies the Stone, according to the current, consensual geological and geographical data (but still told from the heart!).
- **The Physical Integration** — offers how you might identify with the Stone through your body and its instinctual, immediate

language which takes place spontaneously, even when your mind does not seem to know it. If you can absorb that information, then you have just opened your adventure as wide as a dream.

- **The Emotional Integration** — reminds you that your heart, just like the Stones', records everything, feels everything, and then, ultimately, knows everything somehow. This is where you strike gold!
- **Millennial Uses** — shows how you might interpret Stones' ways through the cultures and the consensual reality of humans.
- **Electrical Body Alignment** — acknowledges that we are more than just our physical body, that we have an electrical field around it that receives data far beyond our just-physical senses. This category stirs up that store of knowingness, even when the rest of us didn't even know it was there—that it was us!
- **Affirmation of Support** — bestows upon us an utterly positive chant that we can speak while we are learning so much, so profoundly, that we deserve big support!
- **Stone Story** — directly lands us in the heart of the Stonebeing, itself— one of the generous Stones that guides us beyond our own imagination, on our incredible hobbit's path.
- **Summary** — Yeeeeehaaawwwww! With all this incredible, overflowing, generous information, we are given ONE sentence to sum it up with, so that we can put it in our backpack with all our essential supplies and easily bring it with us on this unknown, loving adventure.

Come along further now, hobbits all................

Then we adventured more deeply into *"Stones Alive! Listening More Deeply to the Gifts of the Earth"* (Volume 2 of the "Stones Alive!" trilogy) and we explored unique Stones from Actinolite to Zircon (along with new, ever more timely energetic Stonecombinations to support we humans). Their energies were downloaded into words to meet us where we now travel our path, with new categories to help us truly absorb the precious Stone gifts:

- **Elemental Earth Grid** — shows the energetic gifts of certain Stones, according to their different geological locations. For instance, Morganite from anywhere brings us sweet compassion, and when it is also specifically Madagascar Morganite, it expresses that compassion through supporting us fulfilling our wishes.

- **Physical, Emotional, Mental Integration** — reminds us that we humans often separate our learning according to our bodies or hearts or minds, alone. Here the Stones invite us to integrate all of that at once, so that we can be magically whole, again.

- **Electrical Body Alignment** — again, acknowledges that we are more than just our physical body, that we have an electrical field around it that receives data far beyond our just-physical senses. This category stirs up that store of knowingness, even when the rest of us didn't even know it was there—that it was us!.

- **Affirmation of Support** — again, bestows upon us an utterly positive chant that we can speak while we are learning so much, so profoundly, that we deserve big support!

- **Dreamtime Doorway** — brings us right into mystery. When you stand at the doorway of mystery with pure willingness, who knows what will happen then? And that's the good news, because you can make anything possible.

- **Stone Story** — directly lands us in the heart of the Stonebeing, itself—one of the generous Stones that guides us beyond our own imagination, on our incredible hobbit's path.

- **Summary** — another Yeeeeehaaawwwww! With all this incredible, overflowing, generous information, we are given ONE sentence to sum it up with, so that we can put it in our backpack with all our essential supplies and easily bring it with us on this unknown, loving adventure.

Now we arrive at the open doorway to the final peaking of this adventure (Go hobbits!!!), *"Stones Alive! Translating the Crystalline Grid,"* (Volume 3 of the "Stones Alive!" trilogy). These generous, Stone-words and ways have evolved to the most current, timely support that they can offer we fast-changing humans. The new categories to organize these gifts for us are:

- **Emotional (Crystalline Grid) Bridge** — walks you right to your, wondrous heart. Sounds simple enough, doesn't it? Yet as we truly begin to heal ourselves— to be our perfection— we often avoid all emotions because we associate them with the source of our pain. It is true: They live at the source of our pain; therefore they also are the source of our healing. When we simply feel all that we are with pure acceptance, as we are kindly, innately, constantly guided to do by the Stonebeings, then we begin walking in full wholeness again. Fortunately for us they travel with us in EVERY adventure— bold or sad— automatically modeling the gloriously unconditional acceptance of the Crystalline Grid...that we all come from...where we all are completely known and loved...where ALL things that happen are just perfect adventures...When you read this, go right to your sweet heart. Feel it. Feel it all. You will be with the Crystalline Grid there, loving it all.

- **Evolutionary Support** — changes and grows with you, in a split second, just as you do. It offers you the strength of the Stones and their timeless wisdom in whatever form you need to translate their gifts to wherever you are traveling now. And as you transform, spontaneously, it will meet you there, too— in a blink! If you try too hard to just "understand" these words, you will miss them on your adventure. Just walk with them. BE them. They are the experience of a lifetime, of many lifetimes— of an Earth evolution.

- **Tools for Co-Creation** — give us practical exercises to absorb the Stonebeings' gifts and make them our loving reality, here and now. If we co-create with the Plants, the Stones, the Animals and the Earth Mother, we will spontaneously co-create a new home that welcomes all of us equally, unconditionally, now.

Yes! We have learned with the Stonebeings, traveling with them through this full trilogy. We are so, so grateful, sharing all of that with you, now. When we co-created the first "Stones Alive!" book, they downloaded us completely with their full vibrations. It took a year and when that blink-of-an-eye time passed, we overflowed with their gifts, spilling them into words, onto pages, in about two weeks. That adventure landed as pure alchemy, turning even our lead into gold. We listened to the Stones and they gave us everything, which we gave to the book. The Stonebeings gave to all of us, utterly.

Then we walked into the adventure of the second "Stones Alive!" book. It was ready for us; we had transformed exponentially from all the listenings of the previous Stone-book. They perfectly met us in our new place of learning and adventure. Rather than simply telling us who and what they are, the Stones urged us to come closer and to listen to them, ourselves. So we did, through the new Stones, the new Stonecombinations, and by listening to them in a new way: Stonefamilies. We and you adventured further, with their hearts encouraging us all the way as we faced new unknowns and new possibilities.

Now we have landed in the culmination of this sweet adventure: the third book in the "Stones Alive!" trilogy. We and the Stones are family, now. In this book-adventure, we and you are listening to the Stones in our own unique ways. It is the season upon the Earth for us to turn those conversations into ways of life— words into reality.

The magic between humans and Stones now lights up our path. All of us can, and are, co-creating with these wise beings. We are co-creating the new world of our dreams. This is the full-out adventure of all these Stone books come together. Join us more and more, please. Let's bring our listening together and translate for the next adventure, the next travelers.

What is the Crystalline Grid and What Does it Mean to Translate it?

The Crystalline Grid is composed of various Stones that make up the structure of the Earth Mother. They are the bones of all matter, shapes, and therefore, also all events occurring here.

Each Crystal and Stone upon the Earth Mother resonates to each other. They echo this vibration through sound, space and light, back to the core of the Earth Mother. This energy echoing back and forth creates a geometric grid. Because the vibrations of the Stones and the core of the Earth Mother are perfectly synchronizing, or they perfectly change to synchronize in a moment, they automatically become a Grid of communication. The vibrations that they are, and that they create together in surrounding all mass here, effectively record every energetic shift no matter how small or large. Every energetic shift creates an action. For humans receiving these vibrations, these actions become events upon which they can offer more actions and responses.

All of this is recorded in the Grid. They are the cells of consciousness. Their continual communication between the core of the Earth Mother and of all Stones vibrates through all matter simultaneously and more or less equally. Because of this, each being upon the Earth Mother then grows in crystalline patterns which then build within their structures their own versions of the Crystalline Grids.

(You might want to go back and re-read this again. It is clear, and ever more so if you choose to believe it but it may be a pattern that you need to repeat to your mind and current belief systems over and over in order for it to embed as a reality structure personally.)

Each Crystalline Grid in each species has traits common to that species but is also slightly unique to each being because every being of each species has its own individual events and stories. So there is a common Crystalline Grid to each species and within that, a unique Grid to each being within that species.

When you harmonize your being to the core of the Earth Mother, your personal Crystalline Grid is activates. There is immediate communication between them that can be consciously translated and utilized. As this occurs in your personal Grid, the Earth's main Crystalline Grid will record all of your individual creations. This is a web of Crystalline consciousness that is completely and fully available to every being upon the Earth. It is evidenced when there is a need simultaneously upon the Earth and various beings in different locations will come up with similar responses or solutions to this need without directly consciously communicating with each other. It is similar to the 100th monkey event.

Animals, plants and minerals automatically, instinctively speak and listen to the Grid with all of their actions. This is true and it is obvious in their automatic behaviors such as bird and whale migration, breeding patterns, and even the mysterious phenomena of whales spontaneously beaching themselves. The most sensitive creature to the Crystalline Grid that we have observed is now the Bottlenose Dolphin, although all whales and dolphins are at the top of the list. However, we have also observed that some of the contributions to the Grid from humans have disrupted some of the harmonious geometries of that same Grid making it difficult for the animals who track by it faithfully.

Humans and the Earth's Crystalline Grid interconnect in different ways from other animal species. Humans learn the language of the Crystalline Grid innately. They add their own (unconscious) understanding to it and not only form their bodies to it but also their personalities, actions, and their cultural structures. They add their unique creations to the Grid which causes the Grid to grow in new ways and formations. Because of their contribution in part, the consciousness of the Earth now extends her Crystalline Grid beyond her body and connects it to ports in this solar system and beyond. She is now securing communications with other types of Grids to root this one more securely to allow for greater growth and even unexpected, unpredictable expansion. It has always been in her consciousness that humans would contribute this. Their exact offerings were not completely predicted, nor could they be or should they be.

The Crystalline Grid is now expanding so that it is multi-dimensionally placed. It is no longer a 3rd dimensional device alone. This means that it receives signals of unexpected origin. The Stonebeings record and record these signals and learn the new languages. The individual Stonebeings according to their own unique gifts are now learning new languages from beyond the Earth. (Look to be aware of new Stonebeings or new finds of previous Stonebeings that are choosing to appear visibly now or to appear in new ways.) They are able to transmit these vibrations here to harmonize the disruptive wave patterns that are often created by uncaring technologies and devices and humans. Even as we speak, there are certain Stonebeings who are transforming the Grid so that with its new vibrations it can literally absorb EMF's and allow them to run through the Van

Allen Belts where they are transmuted and disbursed and even later could be utilized as fuel.

Humans can efficiently utilize the Earth's Crystalline Grid if they fine tune their Grid to consciously receive the ever increasing vibration and therefore gifts of the Earth's Grid. They can learn to create inventions that are not only in harmony with the current vibration but also with the next incoming expanded vibrations. If they do this, it is possible to spontaneously clear the unharmonious effects of previous, uncaring—ultimately disrespectful—technologies.

It is difficult to clear a blocked resonant field from a point within that SAME resonant field. <u>However, if you simultaneously focus on the blockage in the field and have it align with a point from another field that is already cleared, the first resonant field will always attempt to match the harmonious crystallization of the clear field.</u>

This is always true even when it seems to our jumbled human communications that it is impossible.

It is important to remember that all Crystalline Grids immediately form (and keep re-forming) to the most harmonious model available.

This is the ultimate hope for the human species.

In other words, if you can find even (or only) one Crystalline Grid that is primarily clear and functioning gracefully, that Grid will breed throughout the planet spontaneously now, unless there is direct interference from humans. Even then, it cannot be stopped permanently. The clear crystallized patterns of all communications are now transforming and expanding beyond the confusion of humans. It will happen. It is happening.

Your choice is simple. Either you can participate with this or you can attempt to block it, temporarily. The Grid is now mutating more and more rapidly; you know this. It is exponentially forming new Grids with individual Stonebeings who will safeguard them and keep them clear and will also simultaneously align them to clear Grids outside of this planet.

On an individual basis, each human can listen to the Stonebeings who spontaneously clear their own Grids automatically (as all Stones do this), and they can utilize that clarity to spontaneously harmonize themselves with all life geometries upon the Earth, immediately. If they harbor disruptive patterns they can be released according to the need, desire and habits of each human.

There will come a time, and it has already come upon many humans, when our "advanced" technologies will not clear our fields. In other words, they will not heal our diseases, feed our nutritional deficiencies, or harmonize our emotional moods because disruption sometimes breeds more disruption.

Instead, what will heal, feed and harmonize you through your personal and transpersonal existence will be continual contact with clear resonant fields and communication Grids. They will repeat the harmonious flows somewhat like a sacred chant that is continually whispered.

We need to choose to have our bodies, cell by cell, duplicate this perfection and this can happen much more rapidly than our current belief system allows as our human communications are formed from disruption. It is time for us to listen through our own Crystalline Grid, consciously link it to the Earth's, and then to our Solar System's. You/we can align all of our parts of self by doing this far beyond our understanding.

What happens when multiple humans then get together? When multiple humans come together and align their Crystalline Grids, they create beliefs. The quality of beliefs is directly related to the clarity of communication and ease of life geometries between them. Strong beliefs will create Grids that will spontaneously communicate all over the planet at once. Weak beliefs will dominate an area for awhile, but, without ever expanding life geometries, their communications will cycle back on themselves and collapse. The more humans contribute to a common Crystalline Grid, the more efficiently it will create the bulk of structures and organizations that are upon the Earth.

As a human species, we are also integrating contact from extra-terrestrials and from meteorite impacts. They are in our blood and they are in the rivers of the Earth. They are in all structures that make up her body; therefore they are in all structures that make up our bodies and in the structures and organizations that we create here.

This brings us choice in new ways and new levels of support, if we can see to choose them. For many ages, we all have been absorbing the feelings from these contacts and impacts. We have often felt victimized by them and this decreases our ability to act as free beings— almost as if our freedom were irrelevant. The more that we integrate all-that-is with acceptance, the more we are able to wield our freedom, until we are truly free beings.

<u>That is the nature of our life and death choice to incarnate.</u>

Perhaps it has always been before us yet our consciousness now absorbs more freedom and therefore we now can clearly remember the choice to evolve. Therefore, it is before us now, here.

One of the purposes of this book is the clearest possible urging to remember your freedom— and to act upon it, now.

When it comes to freedom, there is only this moment. There is only life. There is only the union with your Spirit standing with you. That is why all things seem so pressing now. It is because freedom is always now. If you do not choose it, you will still have another now and it will only come alive when you choose it. Otherwise, all of your other choices will not come from life. They will not be imprinted from freedom. You can say that you are a free being yet your own choices do not yet make that possible.

Choose your own freedom now. Act with it and through it. All things will answer this brave choice. This complete world and planet will transform now. That is what the Crystalline Grid is whispering to every human whether they are listening or not. Are you listening? It comes to you through the Stones now, to your ears and then to your heart because you have tuned enough of your consciousness to recognize freedom again. This is the moment.

When you listen with these Stones in this book, will you hear, feel, acknowledge, the rememberings of your own freedom? The Stones recorded this for you so that when you were ready, when you had placed aside enough of your own trauma to remember something greater than that, it would all be available to you clearly, simply, now.

As you have already seen in these words, the ability of humans to access and act upon their freedom has increased. That is why the vibration on this planet is so much stronger. This allows greater communication between humans and all others and all other life forms.

There are many ways that perhaps could explain why there is more presence to humans now. Ultimately, it is simply that they have become familiar enough with separation, and also its deadening effects, that they no longer wish to choose this above all else.

It means they must let go of their traumas and grab their own freedom and power instead. They are doing this now. You/we are doing this now. It is why so many things on this planet are so chaotic. We have as a species never really wielded our free power. Therefore it is no surprise that we might not do it easily or completely or gracefully, at first.

We are here. We are speaking with you this way because we know we (and you) are free beings. We know that we/you have power, that we/you can live free. You may need to hear this a great deal like we did (and do) in order to keep reminding you to choose your freedom longer and more than your struggles and pain— just as we have chosen to keep hearing it and living it.

For us, Marilyn and Tohmas, bridging has looked a certain way because everything including our own destiny appears to us according to the parameters of our own consciousness or the space of our acceptance. Up until now our bridging has been quiet, as much in the background as possible. It has meant that we do and be ourselves and this will bridge what we know, what we have learned, to all others.

Everything is changing. The bridging changes too. It now asks us to be more insistent: Louder when need be and to keep repeating the invitation to freedom that is extended to all through their own consciousness. Just as our support repeats this endlessly to us, now we are choosing to do the same. We find more people who wish to hear and a greater depth of listening is available to and from them. This means we must bridge more strongly, more actively, more consciously. It always begins with us, with personal responsibility.

The deeper bridging begins with us. We bridge our own traumas and acceptance and our own freedom with every act. This is not to say that we have not done this, it is saying that we have done this and are doing this, and this allows more life and more freedom to truly do and be all that we have imaged and that our Spirit family invites us to do.

This book is part of our own personal Freedom Intent. It is here to increase the strength of the resonant field of freedom and to support us all in keeping the distractions of separation to a minimum and to keep our focus on respectful communication and to be as clear as possible in all ways. We support this Freedom Intent in how we fuel ourselves and how we practice the whole of our lives. We eat live organic foods only. We drink spring water from our own land. We eat and act slowly and consciously with our focus on digestion of all fuels and with an alignment of simplicity and clarity. We use the tools we have co-created with our Spirits, including our Stonessences, as they seem, for us, to be one of the most efficient, spontaneous healing tools we have. We look to release our oldest traumas and realize we must use all our tools as regularly as possible in order to continue to youthen and regenerate, and we must commit to not repeating the old patterns that continue to create seemingly "new" traumas.

It seems that within this, our human selves, the two-legged part, is the one most of us like and respect the least. Integration comes when we choose to like and respect all things and all parts of self and all else, equally. Like all other beings upon the Earth Mother, we humans offer a purpose and a service. If we cannot see this, or like it, or if it feels impossible, we can still accept it. Just accepting that all the two-leggeds are and do come from the heart of Spirit is healing. Like fear, the parts we all play are mystifying and, at times, not easy in any way but our service is to witness life completely. When there is nothing that we are not willing to witness clearly and compassionately then there will be nothing that we cannot accept. Perhaps the most efficient path to this is letting go of understanding. We don't need to understand anything to accept it. We can just feel this truth and not have to think about it all.

We all at times come to realize that we don't know how to heal. When we realize this, if we can surrender and align with a clear Grid, with Spirit, then we can flow with acceptance and we can freely give ourselves to the biggest picture possible with clear intent.

Here is an exercise to practice living with acceptance:

Reach into your heart and live there completely.

Look around from your heart.

Hear from it.

Taste from it.

Touch from it.

And receive everything of the world in your heart.

Everything that you are is a limb of it.

Now, reach into your life and find what you are feeling and say,

"I FEEL ____________(whatever it is)."

Then absorb it.

Wear it.

Find its texture.

Give it a color.

See how many ways your heart gives and receives one emotion.

When you feel satisfied with its fullness (not necessarily happy, but sated) then say,

"I FEEL ACCEPTANCE."

When there is a great deal going on for you, you can do this. Go into your heart. Do not leave. Find everything it has to express, and say, "I feel hurt." Become it, and say, "I feel Acceptance."

Even when there is not a lot going on, you can do this, spontaneously. Whatever the feeling is, it does not matter whether it is easy or hard or any typically polarized emotion. It is a gift. And when you say, "I feel Acceptance," it becomes a gift that you receive with the openness of your heart.

As you choose to do this regularly, the need for judgment simply slips away.

This practice is also very useful when you do not understand what is happening. You are, at your core, divine, all-knowing beings, and regardless of what you convince yourself that you believe, some of this omni-awareness is with you and is breathing. When you do not understand what's happening, it is often because there is an element of your defenses protecting you from something that you do not fully recognize. On a subconscious level you have given them (the defenses) the authority to supersede most of your processes, and they do. So confusion and not understanding can often mean that some of your defenses are in charge and your conscious self does not know why.

This EXERCISE in/of the heart will accept confusion and go beyond it to the root of what is happening and to what is causing all your different thoughts/feelings. It is simple. And when you add, "I feel Acceptance," to identifying your emotions, you are declaring that it is your Spirit that is in charge, not your judgments or your defenses or separation. You express what is there, what you are giving and receiving, and then you embrace it all. That is why two-leggeds are here on the Earth Mother at all.

The destiny of two-leggeds is to do/be the unimaginable.

Welcome back now from the EXERCISE.

Another way to speak of all of this is in the language of wave patterns.

When an exponential wave pattern (for instance, a clear field) comes in contact with a disruptive wave pattern (for instance, a human in self-judgment) it means that the disruption is exponentially increased and the disruptive wave pattern becomes the variable. The exponential one is free energy at its core and will interact at whatever level of intent is present for the being in the circumstance. It will magnify all the judgments and things that create the circumstance as a disruptive wave pattern.

This creates the opportunity to implode or explode, or to have a clear field, or to make a new choice, or to join with an exponential wave pattern. There is always a single defining moment when we make a change and we move from a disruptive wave pattern to an exponential one.

In the collective memory banks of humans is a belief that change is a dark, long, painful process/event. Because humans are still so much in separation, they allow themselves as a collective conscious to focus on this belief inordinately. That is why the Earth evolution is happening the way it is now. Somewhere along the line people collectively have decided to choose to experience the evolution this way.

Luckily for us, the exponential wave pattern can absorb the disruptive one in/with spontaneous acceptance. This is what the Earth Mother is doing right now. Humans have their own choice in how they will experience this, right now, also. If they choose to focus on their belief in pain and struggle that is how they will be continually experiencing the evolution.

Humans are exponential wave patterns who are holding disruptive wave patterns. This is inexplicable. So what is being asked to happen on a mass level and a personal level is to take beliefs and integrate them with exponential wave patterns. They are called beliefs because we believe in them. This gives the disruptive wave patterns energy and they will color all things and then maintain themselves through repetition. This is why they can seem so overwhelming at times. What makes the integration of the disruptive wave pattern into an exponential wave pattern can be exposing the beliefs as clarity of intent: **The truth is ultimately what fear is most afraid of.**

At this exact moment many humans are on a crash course with all of this and that's where we all are on a collective planetary level. Many/most humans believe in violence because they believe in and are angry at feeling abandoned through separation from the divine, personally and also collectively. This is a huge chip on the collective shoulder and it can color everyone's intent.

Humans will integrate all of this at the level of each single and specific intent. The way integration happens on this level is to repeat and to refine your intent— then some of the disruptive wave patterns are absorbed. For instance, the Stones and Crystals that make up the Crystalline Grid do not choose in the moment to "forget" who they are or what their service is. They continue to hold the clear space/field of consciousness—an exponential wave pattern, regardless of time or weather, or of the stress of humans around them. So they are able to absorb and release disruptive wave patterns in the moment.

Our evolution as humans does not have to be earned or

willed— we choose it by intending it. We believe our beliefs because we believe they are true and we have a long-standing belief that this has to be a long, drawn-out struggle. If we all realized how this colored our intent, personally and collectively, we might all be more careful in each belief. We might also pay more attention to not REABSORBING all the disruptive wave patterns floating around. The Elementals, the Devic spirits of the four elements that comprise all matter on the Earth: Air; Fire; Earth; and Water—the core of the Crystalline Grid—are always clearing disruptive beliefs, because they can become addictions and we all know how challenging it is in the collective wave patterns of humans to give up addictions.

Our job is to keep our intent clear at all times. This has to be front and center in our consciousness. You can go to your disruptive wave patterns now and repeatedly and offer them acceptance—a new way of life, a new energy.

It doesn't matter if you believe the change, initially, or not. Of course the disruptive patterns are not going to believe the new intent. It's always up to you to decide how you want to spend your time here on the Earth Mother. You need to keep making the new affirmations and intents. We all have to keep going back to them for them to embody, for them to "take": Like attracts like. Your old beliefs will cloud your ability to manifest through your new intent. You need to stay committed, insistent. Eventually the disruptive patterns will be absorbed by the exponential ones and they won't have the same focus. When enough people do this, the collective disruptive patterns can be absorbed and changed, also.

Our new beliefs create our new bodies which are wired to exponential wave patterns. The old bodies were wired to disruptive patterns connected to unconscious death. New bodies are linked to immortality (conscious life with full acceptance). If you want to know how to absorb exponential wave patterns, go to your body. It has recorded it all and retains the cellular memory of it. If you exit or abandon your body, you are absorbing disruptive wave patterns. Your body knows where the disruptive patterns reside even though your mind will try to hide them. The body holds all the energy wave patterns you have ever experienced: It is your Crystalline Grid. It is the Crystalline Grid.

In one sense, the Crystalline Grid is the space between the disruptive wave pattern and the exponential wave pattern. It is there and accessible so you can absorb, if you choose, the exponential wave pattern as respectfully and as compassionately as possible. We are being called to fine-tune the body and recognize it for what it is: **It is the practical bridge between you and everything you have ever been and ever will be.** It is modeled after the Earth Mother. Spirit creates your body in her likeness. To some humans she is the enemy: wild, and able to kill you, limited with resources, etc., because these are the beliefs that get birthed from an addictive personality. The way that people respond to the Earth is the same way that people respond to their bodies, and vice versa. This is the playing field where we choose to act out our own unique journey with Spirit. It doesn't have to be with limits. These beliefs that the body is limited or bad are what keep us separate from Spirit. If body equals separation, then this belief of separation is good cause to fight your own body.

Actually, at any given moment, most human beings are not even in their bodies. They may leave behind 5% or so when they vacate, but they tend to leave behind the nasty parts, the defenses. When met with the unexpected or the unknown, most humans choose to vacate and to let their defenses rule. The Crystalline Grid, a clear, exponential wave pattern, invites us to fully inhabit our own divine/mortal vessels, our bodies, and all that comes along with them, in order to consciously evolve with the Earth Mother. Only an exponential wave pattern can bridge between a disruptive wave pattern and an exponential wave pattern.

To support all of us in these challenging times and amidst our own personal traumas and the seeming larger ones we have all created together, the wisdom of the Stonebeings and the Crystalline Grid comes to us simply, Elementally, to help us evolve—as immortals have known throughout time and timelessness. Timelessness is the link between immortality and time. It is our opportunity to link all Ages with our actions now and our Beingness/Intent. In other words, every two legged is timeless according to how they use their consciousness. If you use it in the little picture only, if you spend it on regret, fear and judgment, then it will fade away in the wind when your body does go back to the Earth Mother. If you use your consciousness to join with the bigger picture, if you spend it with love, freedom and joy, then every act is for all Beings in all times in all spaces. It is the only complete way we know of to heal.

So the Elementals have given us these rooted and grounded attributes/practices to support us on our journey.

The four attributes of co-creating with the Elementals:

1.) **Always travel with your own Sacred Witness.** Always come back to it. It is an emptying and a heart opening. This means that you are always connecting with Great Spirit and the biggest picture of life possible. It means that in all your choices you consider all beings, not just yourself. However, you also need to realize that you are as important a consideration in your big picture as any other being. Your Sacred Witness represents freedom, equality, respect and enlightenment. Its key practice for you is detachment. Its Elemental Guardian is the Air Element.

2.) **Always ground your chosen reality deep into the Earth Mother.** Ask yourself, "Is this what I am choosing? Am I in harmony with all parts of myself?" Every two legged, every moment, faces unlimited choices. It is exciting. It is overwhelming. It is a miracle. However, because two leggeds have come here to learn separation they do not ground their truth very often. The unlimitedness of choice in life tends to boggle them. So your task is to embrace the limits of separation by declaring your life, your choices, every moment. More than that, when you intend your life, immediately root it into the Earth Mother. This act embraces separation and connects it to UNION. This attribute's Elemental Guardian is Earth.

3.) **Do everything each moment with respect, clarity and efficiency.** This is the evidence of compassion for everything. While it is innately within you, this quality is sleeping most of the time because of the primary learning of separation we all have chosen. If you act with respect, clarity and efficiency it will awaken your true nature. It will allow you to be in immediate contact with all beings and their hearts. This attribute's Elemental Guardian is Water.

4.) **Change.** As often as you can, become family with change. It is the language of this time, a season of change. To change every moment is the natural flow of life. Again, because of attachment to separation your transformative qualities are sleeping a bit. Awaken them. Change constantly. Change whenever you think of it even if you don't know what to change or how. You can even practice changing before you are ready to do so but have already been feeling the need. Change, and your willingness to always be it, places you in the stream of life. This attribute's Elemental Guardian is Fire.

5.) We invite you, as Spirit did/does with us to add a fifth attribute here for yourself. **It is Mystery.** We do not, nor can we, guide you in it, it will be whatever you choose. If we speak too much of it, the magic will begin to shape and it prefers to do that itself. This attribute's Elemental Guardian is Ethers.

Attributes 1 & 2 are the ATTRACTERS, calling forth from Spirit what you don't even know you need.

Attributes 3 & 4 are the MANIFESTERS that go beyond yourself but are grounded in the Sky and the Earth and become evolution instead of unintended desire.

As you choose to live timelessness in time, we invite you to bring along the Elementals by speaking their language- action. The first two are visionaries. They allow you to connect with your own Spirit so that you can attract everything spontaneously that you need and want. The second two are manifesters. You must practice them every single moment. Once you have attracted anything, you can offer them the two manifester attributes. This will continually shape the reality you wish to co-create with the Elementals and the Crystalline Grid.

As we also look down on the Earth Mother with an Eagle, Hawk, or Butterfly eye, we can see that each direction of the Earth Mother corresponds to a very basic Elemental from which the Beings there build/manifest from at this particular time.

In the **Northwest**, the Air Elemental lays out the basic intent that will reflect the need for breathing, communication, learning, freedom, and curiosity. The humans whose geometries correspond to this are ever looking for ways to bring their humanness into strength or domination with the Earth Mother and its Beings. They are fond of words and inventions and great speed.

The North American continent, the United Kingdom, Europe, and Scandinavia represent the **Northwest** direction Elementally, currently. Greenland and Iceland also participate but they hold less of the human Air qualities.

Stonebeings to work with and open your heart to in relation to the **Northwest** direction are all Lemurian Seed Crystals and all Calcites, and then it becomes very unique to different areas and different evolutions. The Air imprint (as are all of the Elemental imprints) is basic. It is a foundation. It is so omnipresent, it is not very specific. The Stonebeings are evolving and changing and are inviting us now to move and change and co-create with them. We invite you in this book to go deeper with your own questioning and listening to find these more specific layers for yourself in co-creating with the specific Stonebeings.

The **Southwest** direction bears the imprint of Fire. The land and the Stones there bring forth a pure creativity. They answer life with spontaneous art. They teach us how to enjoy all things, big or small. They are immediate with their passions and they must learn of change.

The **Southwest** direction is represented by the South American continent, the Central Americas, the Caribbean, Africa, the Middle Eastern areas, and the Mediterranean areas.

Stonebeings to work with and open your heart to in relation to these areas are Carnelians, Jaspers, and Agates.

The **Northeastern** direction bears the imprint of Earth. There is a rootedness in learning about how the Earth Mother works and plays and designs her creations. There is a constant movement towards balance, unhurriedness, and understanding. Here there can be a great appreciation for all experiences of life.

The **Northeastern** direction is represented by Eastern Europe, western Asia, Russia, northern China and its surrounding territories.

Stonebeings to work with and open your heart to in relation to this area are Smokey Quartz, Lingams, and Obsidian.

The **Southeastern** direction bears the imprint of Water. It remembers from the heart. It lives with emotions. It seeks the flow of all things, joining. It is the most omnipresent of the

Elements upon the Earth. And so, it carries the rhythm of the evolution of the Earth Mother.

The **Southeastern** direction includes the Orient, eastern Russia, southeastern Asia, India, all South Pacific areas, Australia and New Zealand, and unknown parts of the Earth.

Stonebeings to work with and open your heart to in relation to this area are Gemstones, Lasers, and Water Stones such as Pearls and Coral.

The **Polar** directions, the Arctic and the Antarctic, carry an imprint of the Air meeting the Ethers, where balance is allowed between the Earth Mother and all beings with a different focus than anywhere else upon the Earth Mother.

Stonebeings to work with and open your heart to in relation to this area are any Stones that are available to you in the moment, as this area can adapt to any circumstance spontaneously.

Choose to remember now that the Crystalline Grid is available to all beings upon the Earth, and this includes YOU. Whenever you root, you can reach it and it will tell you whatever is happening upon the Earth and, if you wish, what is happening with your own specific body. Though humans think they do not know it, the Grid links all of them. It is how we all belong here. It is the original blueprint of bodies on the Earth and so it is the blueprint for manifesting form.

When you root into the Crystalline Grid consciously, it activates the Grid within you. It reminds you of the bigger picture of life as you are manifesting your own individual and unlimited life. When the inner and outer Grids are active simultaneously, the consensual two-legged linear paradigm is not so dominant. It is still there if and when you need it; yet, it no longer is in charge of your nervous system (for that is how it operates).

When you are very small, everything is communicated to you but it is derived from separation so it cannot be in all of your chakras as the moving lifeforce that it could be. Separation cannot be fully grounded in you or in your root. Instead, it is imprinted on the nervous system so that it will be an alert system. It will let you know when to fear. It will focus on this because it cannot be completely grounded.

The paradigm of separation simply cannot communicate with all that you are. It is not designed that way. When you fully listen to the Crystalline Grid, it is already a part of you. It is designed that way. It is family. It will communicate with all that you are and you will not necessarily be aware of all of it. Instead, you will feel it as it balances out your needs and then lands upon what it is that will most nourish you now. **It will focus, not on what it wants to tell you, but what you are ready to listen to with as much of your being as possible.**

The Crystalline Grid speaks to this and in this way. That's what you will feel. It is as if it answers you before you ask any questions. It is utterly immediate and respectful. It will not seek you out, for it already knows you and knows where you are. If you are already listening to the ways of separation, it will not interrupt your learning. The Grid simply records everything without judgment. And when you are ready for something else, when you crave a different conversation, it will be ready. It will shape exactly to your needs, not necessarily to your wants, for sometimes they are the unsatisfied children of your attachment to lack.

The Crystalline Grid so knows you. It will speak directly to what will most support you, even if you do not know it or recognize it. That is why, to most two-leggeds, it is only a whisper among howling winds.

You must go to it if you want to live with its wisdom by your side. You must choose it. You must gather together all your intent and offer it to the Grid. Tell it from your heart how you wish to connect with it now. Then you can hear it. You can listen with it. And when you listen with the Crystalline Grid, you will hear it listening to all life. You will hear every bird's song. You will know all the cares and secret delights of every child upon the Earth Mother. Everything is utterly nurtured here that has been created under the Sky Father upon the Earth Mother. Your defenses will deny this and say that the Grid does not care. And it seems this way in some moments, because judgment is completely absent from its makeup.

While it is steady and grounded, the Grid attaches to nothing. It is true that when you come to it, you can come and go as you wish completely and unlike beings of separation, the Crystalline Grid will not make you do anything. It will simply be with you forever no matter what dimensions you explore. The imprint of the Grid can always be yours if that is your free choice. You simply must join with it in the way that it offers itself to you-free, unjudged, unconditional.

Perhaps the most immediate way to go to the Grid and to be with it is to let the noise of the outside world not rest upon you. Be like the Grid. Record its visits but attach to none of it. Then you will find yourself at the Center Stillness because that's all that is left when you pull away the distractions and the noise in your life. Join your Center Stillness with that of the Grid.

Be as one being.

Breathe together.

Everything will come to you.

Everything will be offered.

Some of it will stir you beyond imagination. Some of it will explode your expectations and disillusionments.

Just be and be and be.

Absorb your union. You are both a part of the Earth and you are meant to know each other as much as your willingness will allow.

Be conscious.

And live with the Grid every moment that it occurs to you. This will ground your body and your toes into a reality that your parents may not have taught you. Really no one can teach it. You can only go to it of your own acceptance, or not.

The more consciously you walk grounded in the Grid, your inner Grid will also activate. If you do this enough, it will quietly and necessarily replace the separation in your nerves. You will be rooted instead of cut off. Everything will change.

There is no way to put words upon this even though we are so let's pause now and journey directly to the heart of the Crystalline Grid.

You will need to be grounded, feet on the floor and breathing. (You might want to ask a friend to read this journey for you so you can completely immerse yourself in it, and then return the favor so your friend can do the same.)

Take however much time you need to feel complete before you read on.

Now take my hand (I am a Stonebeing.).

We can travel the full inside of the Earth Mother together.

I will not make you do this.

I will not show you how to do it my way.

Instead, I will travel with YOU because I know that within your being you do this innately.

I know we can travel your intent together as easily as a single moment of clear thought.

I will pause here for a moment so that you can consciously verbalize your respectful desire in how you will enter the heart of the Earth Mother.

Now we are free and we are joined.

I am a Crystalline Being. All that I am is intent that is recorded upon every cell and then also echoed upon the Crystalline Grid.

You are a Crystalline Being, who for a short breath or two, seems to forget the very nature of your Crystalline Beingness. I know the key that you have been seeking, even when you have given up seeking.

You are looking for the Crystalline Grid. You know that when you touch it, it and you, will reorganize matter. You will transmute the shape and the movement of your cells according to whatever intent you held dear when you touched the Grid.

Connecting with the Grid sharpens your focus.

It allows all of your thoughts and feelings and passions to come to a single point.

You remember how to utilize all of your vast powerful and scattered resources.

You are a Crystalline Being as well.

You now travel your intent into the Earth Mother.

Make yourself free to simply do and be this now. As you wish, everything else will wait.

For to do this with focus will realign and reconnect the inherent energies within you.

Close your eyes.

Open your heart.

Blossom your third eye.

See and feel it revolving and spinning in your head identifying energy that has seemingly eluded you until now.

This metaphysical eye is your guide.

It is the shaman of your journey.

Breathe from this eye downward through all of your cells into the roots below your feet.

It is natural.

It is ease.

I will Om in the background.

You can join me so that as unneeded thoughts arise they can freely leave through the Om to their next shape and service.

Grow your roots as far into the Earth Mother as she allows.

Through them, be and smell the underground rivers and caves.

Touch the roots of mountains.

The vastness is unlimited.

Pick a home of your own choosing.

You can live on the Grid or within a gigantic Crystalline cluster or simply be in the Earth, quietly gestating.

Choose.

Focus.

All your energy follows.

Your home is here and now.

You have brought me along as witness.

I record this within my Quartz which imprints the Grid with your journey.

It is not simply a dream or an image.

It is your joining with the union that is the Earth Mother.

Ommmmmmmmmmm.

Personal Story

We are Stone listeners. We talk with them every day, just like you talk with your friends, or your family. They are family to us and we love every part of it.

In listening with the Stones for this book, we have learned so much more than we ever knew was possible. Some of it has been a very tall mountain to climb. We have been given many opportunities to act upon our true divinity. It is beyond glorious. It is a pure dream that just walks right into our life and makes itself so.

Lately we have been listening with the Crystalline Grid (just like you!). It powerfully breaks us open and sets us free. Our Spirits tell us that this is the season that holds the potential for the biggest, most immediate evolution for our species. To say that we are feeling that in our hearts and in our struggles and unlimited hopes would be a chasm of an understatement.

Every day, the Crystalline Grid (or some generous part of it, like Grandfather Lingam) shows us the big picture of the overnight transformation that we two-leggeds are, or are just about to be. It astounds us. We cry at the constant, sheer glory of it. Here we are watching it . . . clearly . . . consciously . . . just as our Spirits have ever intended, beyond time and space and dreams and even landing right into them, too. It is the vision-come-true that we almost didn't dare to dream.

So we are growing stronger and braver than previously imaginable. Simultaneously, the deepest, buried fears have arisen as tall as those mountains. They loom before us on our path, demanding finally to be loved before we can go on, before we can evolve into the pure magnificence that we can already SEE just ahead of us—taunting us into more.

Some days, we practice what was previously unimaginable. People talk to us and the sages in us come out and they see as clearly as crystal balls. We are living the truth. Other days, we're barely crawling, we're so low. It exhausts us to live with such fullness, with such bright colors of joy and grief, all wrapped together in the transformation that is us. It is us.

Writing "Stones Alive! 3" has been profoundly different than the first two books, which just seemed to automatically birth themselves. With this one, so many more things were happening in our life and sometimes, everything else going on seemed almost like impossible distractions—like they were making it hard to ever get the book done. As ever, we just kept listening and kept acting upon the wisdom of the Stonebeings, who just quietly encouraged us. They let us know that the book was still forming and growing, amongst everything else. And they would know—they are the timelessly patient recordkeepers of all. We trust them. We always trust them, but we could feel the pushing of their creativity on our shoulders and it just seemed like we couldn't make it happen fast enough.

During this book-journey, a friend of ours asked if she could birth her child, at our primitive mountain home and oasis. We listened to our Spirits and the Spirit of the unborn child, and they both said, "Yes," so we said, "Yes" too. What else is there? It was utterly thrilling and simultaneously exhausting, happening at the exact time we had already committed to as a deadline for the new book. We gave unlimited time and energy to supporting and doing whatever was necessary and respectful; sometimes it stole all our time from Stone listening— at least for a while. We had to do it. We didn't fully understand it, yet that just isn't our biggest criteria. We are here to act upon our Spirits. Sometimes a driving need to "understand" just makes acting more of a struggle. So we helped to birth the miracle of Kahlill (the new baby), while the next pages of the book just laid open and silently empty.

In the midst of all of this, the Crystalline Grid kindly spoke to us:

The loving vibration on the Earth Mother moves and shifts so easily and so exponentially now. She is evolving. She is evolving within her own consciousness and within the universe that she lives and breathes in. The Earth is constantly expanding her energy into space, which means that simultaneously she must grow her roots more deeply and generously within, as well.

As she stretches, every being upon her feels this. For those of you who listen to her, you will truly stretch, far beyond the human world of rationality and expectations. For ages you have lived upon her and you have evolved certain structures of reality and of how to cope with them well. You know how to add numbers. You know how to measure possibilities. You do your best to fit your life well into time and you try to explain the mysteries of the universe with cause and effect, through trial and error. These have worked for you. You have learned so much and you have done so much, and you keep learning and doing.

Yet you accomplished all of this before the new, current vibration of the Earth. As her hertz rise and her magnetics fall, the resonant field that you have played and worked on has changed. So you must change all expectations and your creativity to fit this new structure. And the way to fit with it is to lose your expectations, so that you are openly free to actually watch the cycles of life and learn directly from them. They are what most affects you; your will cannot match that. Put aside the massive intellect that you have developed. It is impressive, but it doesn't match a world that leads by its heart. To manifest with this new vibration upon the Earth Mother, you must feel first and then let thinking fill the other gaps. To feel your way, you must listen first and then match your heart to the Earth's heart and evolve with her, not against her.

You are listening with us now. So we will tell you. You have been pushing too hard. Putting more and more effort into your work sometimes echoes the old human paradigm of lack and unanswered need. Everything is coming to you. It is coming to you so abundantly, it will stun you in your steps. Place your energy into receiving, as well as giving. Balance will bring you more when you actually need it, not when you are only afraid that you need it.

To write this book with the Stones, you must dive into the new Earth vibration and swim in it. It must be with you in every word, on every page. It's not possible to write the book and THEN listen to the evolving Earth energy. You must do it while you are listening and writing and that will not fit into the former time parameters you already understand. You are growing NEW parameters. For you this is the hard news and the best news. It will not calm your fears; it will grow your strength right over the top of them, while they are still crying.

We couldn't talk with you about this before now, until you had already tasted the newest vibration (which has you reeling), so that you could truly feel, heart to roots, all of what we are offering. Go and be a part of the child birthing at your home. Heal yourselves as your anger explodes and sputters out festering frustrations. Do all the things that seem to take you away from us, from our listenings. Be them. Just be them with the new Earth vibration now.

When you are done smoothing some of the cracks in your Shields, when you are done welcoming baby Kahlill, the words that we will co-create together will carry the newest, most unimaginable gifts from us and from the Earth

Mother. You won't recognize that— you won't be able to prove it yet— but one day all of this will be so much a part of you that these words and ways that you are still initiating within will be like your thumbs. They will go with you everywhere and they will be your immediate tools long before you think to examine or understand them.

This is what you have to offer. It is simple, but it is not easy. You are bridges. You bridge between humans and all other lifeforms on the Earth Mother and you must wear all those vibrations through your own human bodies before they will be able to translate between those dimensions. When you have walked in all those worlds, yourselves, then whatever words come through you will carry the new Earth vibration as a simple, free gift. All humans who are willing can partake of it, as easily as they wish.

Yes.

We accept it. We accept it all and we trust that one day it will make sense to all parts of us after we have evolved and keep evolving. It is the path that our Spirits have asked us to walk and we are doing it right now. It has not always been easy to write this book, and it's not fun sharing all of our struggles and our perfect weirdness so transparently, but here they are. It is what we have to offer. "Stones Alive! 3" is more of a co-creation than any of its predecessors and here's why: There is more of us in it. We, as humans, are stepping up to the plate and sharing as freely as the Stones ever have.

We trust that you will feel this. We invite you to accept it all as a pure gift, even if it is not quite for you. It is all that we have to give and we give it with all our hearts.

~Marilyn and Tohmas T.

2,000 pound, 7 foot tall, Shiva Lingam now standing in Silver City, New Mexico. This is the first Lingam to be placed in our new international program spearheaded by our non-profit, Elementals of Life, linking Lingams and the Crystalline Grid and humans with the intent and focus of Respect for all Life as a Way of Life. With the Lingams support, we are grounding the new Earth Paradigm where all Beings- Plant, Animal & Mineral live together in harmonious, equal freedom and co-creativity.

Whisperings......

Do you know that the inside of the Earth
is like the inside of your own body?
You have blood like rivers
and bones like mountains.
Deep inside the Earth there lives a grid,
an endless, underground geometry of all her crystals
that speaks across the expanse of canyons, caves and oceans.
It tells her all events and all thoughts and feelings
immediately, clearly.
Do you hear it?
When you quiet your struggle
do you hear the inner Earth whispering,
constantly praising every tree
constantly celebrating every storm?
The whispers, the praise, the celebrations
come to you constantly
echoing across your blood rivers and bone mountains.
They whisper the treasures
of watching life stretch and shudder and soften
each moment.
All this lands softly upon us.
The Crystalline Grid records it all.
This quiet bounty opens itself to the children of Earth now.

Stones A - Z

A few words, again, about the Physical Descriptions of the following Stonebeings.

As you well know if you have read Stones Alive!, Volumes 1 and/or 2, we are Storytellers not scientists. We do not pretend to know much of anything. We offer our hearts, our stories and the stories of the Stonebeings

The information in the Physical Descriptions that follow for each Stonebeing are gleaned from multiple sources including the internet and we simply present this information as common knowledge that you can use or not use as you choose.

We also invite you to believe or not believe it as you choose. As we all know, the Earth Mother is constantly shifting and evolving and everything changes constantly, as much as some science and technology likes to resist those changes when they do not suit or seem to support its already stated purposes.

Try to focus on listening to what is in your heart when you read these descriptions and then take from them what serves you best so you can go on to see and feel and hear and sense all things surrounding the experience and adventure of these live Beings, not just what you are told is so or has to be. Your experience, again, is what is most important. Not what we say or write. If your experience is different than what you find written here, we joyfully acknowledge that and you and welcome that information as a vital, living part of the Crystalline Grid that is perfect, useful and appreciated. Send us your stories.

Do what you can, when you read the Physical Descriptions, to listen to and respect the voices that are speaking and then honor your own heart voice first within that respectful listening and right relationship. You do not need to spend too much time getting caught up in the details (unless that is fun for you) as they are simply presented. You can find

Personal Story

Arizona Sunstone

Escaping a heat wave in central Arizona in mid-July, I left for a camping trip to the pine forest in eastern Arizona above 7,000 feet with ample streams, lakes and cool shade. I left late in the day and the ensuing 5 hour drive assured setting up camp in the dark. I traveled down a two track dirt road late in the volcanic basalt flows and cinder cone studded terrain of this remote Arizona/New Mexico border.

The last barbed wire gate leading to my desired campsite lay ahead. My headlights caught an elk herd paralleling the fence. I shut off the headlights to observe the elk in the moonlight. While walking back to close the last gate, I glanced to the ground drawn by the glimmer of many Sunstones reflecting the moon and starlight back into the heavens. It looked like pieces of heaven trapped on the Earth. The next day I returned to the fence line to gather all the little bits of heaven.

~Robert P.

endless details and versions thereof in so many other places (and we truly honor the validity and usefulness of those details.). We invite you here to accept that for what it is and move easily and gracefully on to how the Stonebeings choose to tell their own stories as Evolutionary Support and Tools for Co-creating. It is all a part of what is, but where we continually choose to place our focus will determine, largely, what is or becomes visible or invisible in the practice of our daily lives.

We invite you to keep coming back to placing your focus on the heart of the matter, the currents that flow with the Story, so you then can find for yourself the integrations, physical, mental, emotional, that lie waiting within the words that follow.

~Welcome~

Albite

I am Sodium, Calcium, Aluminum and Oxygen. I am sometimes synonymous with Clevelandite. My name comes from the Latin, Albus, alluding to a common color. I am usually colorless to white but can tend towards bluish, greenish, grey and I have a hardness of 6 to 6.5. I can form in blocky tabular crystals and am widely distributed.

Emotional (Crystalline Grid) Bridge: Together we feel purity so long, so thoroughly that you center in your original innocence. Now look at the world! You are a child, and not a child as you were (learning separation)— you are a child who is reaching into divinity after having seen what life is like without even the taste of it.

I sharpen your smell, when need be, so that your memories will all come back to your innocent divinity. Everything you remember can be from that.

Evolutionary Support: Welcome. I come to you to refine what you are doing. You are a divine being (even during your struggles) and that never leaves you.

It never goes away.

Embrace that and everything you do changes. It simply changes and there is no way for you to predict that. You are creating a new world.

Tools for Co-Creation

Smile.
It is not so hard to work and play with Stones.
If it was, you wouldn't even be here.
We have grown up together— our species— on this planet, although

my species is a bit older.......

We can join anytime you wish, because of that.

How would you like to make magic together?

Once you fully intend what you wish to do
from your heart,
everything else will answer that,
including me.

Alexandrite

As I am spoken of here, I am usually found in Brazil or Russia. I am an interesting crystal in that on the surface I can appear very dark and grey, green or black. But shine a light through my crystals and you see my color change to deep, deep red. I am a form of Chrysoberyl and have been named in honor of Alexander II, Czar of Russia from 1855-1881.

Emotional (Crystalline Grid) Bridge: Transformation. I touch transformation in you. Now come to my heart. Can you find it in my reflection? We are phoenixes, butterflies, the Earth Mother evolving right now. Burn and arise from the ashes, as an adventure!

Evolutionary Support: My heart is aglow! So is yours. Do you see it, do you touch it? It brings in mighty lifeforce to care for even the tiniest cell of you. It awaits all parts of you to recognize the innocent, incredible power it has through love.

Tools for Co-Creation

Many Stones love to be close to you in some way.
I love being close to you
in any way you choose.

I know that your journey has been full of hurts and confusion
that shape you.
They twist you around until you cannot see straight.

I'm patient (but excited!).

Come to me when and how you can.
Once we are together, I will touch your heart and proclaim it as the might that it is!

When I am nearby, or when you hear of me, pause a moment.
Think of all the ways that you have been brave
just being you.

I will grow and soar your thoughts into a powerful foundation
for wondrous life and for
dreams-coming-true!

Andara

I have been said to resemble crystalline glass lava. Much has been written about me and I suggest you search on the web for the easily obtainable multiple writings and decide for yourself what I truly am in your own heart. I truly resemble glass lava and I come in many colors. There are also now multiple find locations. Again, I ask you to decide for yourself the truth and the pertinence of these writings and finds.

We (Marilyn and Tohmas) remind you that our job is only to LISTEN to these Beings themselves and pass on directly their story, not to judge or decide for you what is real. Remember that everything is present in the Crystalline Grid. From that focus, we choose then how we utilize and act upon what is present through our focus and intent.

Emotional (Crystalline Grid) Bridge: I say nothing. Let me hold your struggle. Let me shout your bliss! Let me stand beside you so that you might know a smile when you are so alone that you hear nothing, no one, but fear overruling your love.

Evolutionary Support: I am here to show you that you are made of so many things. To you those things are all so vastly different that sometimes you can't see how they come together, or even why they should.........but they do. All you need to know is that all the different parts of life come together in you. They live in you. They tell you everything. They sing whenever you listen.

Tools for Co-Creation

I am a magical being.
You are a magical being.
Our differences bring us together.
The sameness that results from this is
magic.

Do you take that for granted?

Then wake up brand new!
Hold me just once (That's all you will need.).
Now carry my awakening song in your heart.
Wherever you go, whatever you do,
find the magic.
Open your eyes so brimmed-wide that you see it everywhere.

Whenever you find the magic,
Pause.
Take in a very full, delighting breath.
Breathe out big, loud, and strong and say,
"I accept the magic of Andara within me and I offer it to you now.
Together we co-create magic."

Watch. Listen. More magic will answer.
More and more magic will show you the ways of co-creation
as different and as the same
as all of us.

Personal Story

ANDARA— the light of beauty and perfection

This unique glassy substance has been for me a catalyst of very unusual and beautiful change. It has always been a vehicle of manifestation for me and seems to lead me to forging new friends and adventures. My first introduction to this mysterious mineraloid was right before a seminar on formations of the quartz crystal. An old friend introduced one of her newer acquaintances to me and excitedly added, "She's got a crystal for you to meet..." Of course I was eager.

Andara was the name of this lavender lump of glassy material. She started a far-fetched story of Lemuria and made mention of it coming from California. Though open-minded, I approach things with caution, and Andara was no different. It was purple glass. My expectations were nothing near what I felt. The moment I held the stone and followed my new acquaintance's directions for merging with it, I was overcome with this surging feeling. Energy anchored into me and amazed me.

I had to have some.

Not long thereafter I followed my intuition and got a couple of green pieces within my budget, but since that time, I have been lucky to work with lots more in personal sessions, workshops, meditations, and on my own. I soon learned of another good source of info and contacted her. I offered to study any material I could get my hands on at the local mineral museum in which I worked, so she sent me some pieces. The refractive indices and dispersal ratios are much higher than plain old glass, and the energy is always astounding. She even sent me some of the more difficult to acquire Andara hailing from Indonesia.

In the midst of my Andara journeys, I was given a tip-off about the potential location for more Andara, this time minutes away from my hometown of Stuart, FL. While it is not known whether the Californian material is natural, this location would most definitely be the result of human activity. Skeptical again, I followed my inner guidance. After some exploring we tested all of the recovered glass in the many hues of green, clear, blue, and lavender. The darkest browns seemed to give off the strongest energy at first, but later each stonebeing seemed to awaken and begin its personal journey. Many pieces that my friends and I found have since made their way around the world.

The different forms of Andara seem to love to be together. I often feel guided to include them from all three locations I have collected to generate a beautiful synergetic embrace; it carries the symbolism of bringing all peoples together to embrace our mutual beauty, power, and love.

Interestingly enough, many pieces of Andara will fluoresce when exposed to a shortwave UV lamp, or sometimes even a blacklight. They seem to bend a lot of rules, since glass is traditionally nonreactive and even insulates and filters out UV energy.

Andara has always spoken so clearly to me about personal change and responsibility. It seems to work on such a deeper soul level than many of my other crystalline friends, even though it lacks the long-range order of a true mineral. It seems that Andara has a very unique message for the new millennium, and that it speaks it to one soul at a time. For me, Andara guides me on my path of personal evolution, and I truly feel drawn to share it everywhere I go. As one of the highest frequencies I have used in crystal healing, Andara has helped with manifestation through sacred sound, increases receptivity to «paranormal activity,» and feels as though it literally changes auric fields when carried or worn. Andara has become a sort of personal totem stone, and it has been one of those stones that I can always return to in order to remind me of the potential within.

~Nick P.

Atacamite

I am named after my find location, the Atacam Desert Province in northern Chile. I am very green and am similar in ways to Malachite and Dioptase. I am a secondary mineral of Copper especially formed in arid, saline areas. I am soft and brittle and usually form in very small crystals.

Emotional (Crystalline Grid) Bridge: We are home

There is a deep, magical root into the absolute center of the Earth Mother here; our coming together in pure willingness has turned it from what used to be an invisible wish from your Etheric memories to a full-dream-come-true-now.

Let's climb it to the core. We will bring along adventurer fears and excitement to honor the center of the Earth Mother and the center of ourselves and our once invisible impossibilities and our once unspoken dreams.

Ohm...................

Evolutionary Support: I am underlying, in-between, slipped-in-the-side support. In the Earth Mother, I form with other Stones and chemicals to make whatever is needed, wherever it is needed.

When I am with humans, you may not notice me. I softly blend with everything. I support all that is. If you are letting go of pain, I gentle that release. If you are dancing with joy, I lift you off the ground, into..............

Tools for Co-Creation

There are seasons for everything.
Anything that you want to learn will offer itself to you
at the perfect moment
in the perfect place.

If you don't know that, it is simple: You are learning acceptance.
It is making itself available to you
right now.
It is speaking through my voice
and echoing in our joined hearts (and yes yes, our hearts are joined.).

If you still do not know that
it is because you believe that trust hurt you somehow.
I understand.

Yet I am still speaking through that hurt—
beyond it—
to your heart: **You are acceptance.**
The rest of you is still learning it.

That is why I am here.

Axinite

I am usually a translucent brown and am also usually found as fero-Axinite due to my common occurrences with Iron. I can also be found more rarely with Magnesium and Manganese. I can be found most often in North America, Europe and Australia. My brown color can move into pale greens and blues and even yellows, and my name in part comes from the Greek word, "acine," or "ax," which refers to the acute shape of how I typically crystallize.

Emotional (Crystalline Grid) Bridge: Clarity is everywhere. It is everything. All of life dances itself to us in myriads of faces, happenings and senses.

If you're not seeing it, then I'm with clarity knocking at the door of your heart, smiling gently saying, "Open up. Open up, now. Stay open......"

Evolutionary Support: I know your world. It overflows with stimuli and ideas. It thrills you, but sometimes it charges like an onslaught that you can't manage.

I go to the core of everything— this helps you to ground your body and be present, not overwhelmed.

I choose awareness— this helps you to consider what you truly want, instead of letting yourself be carried away in a flood of others' desires, needs and attention-getting shows.

I am with you, as I am with everything: I bring all of myself. Then I can give and receive the precise gifts that Spirit imbued in me to give to and to receive from the beautiful wheel of life.

Tools for Co-Creation

In other times (sometimes less frenetic ones), people knew that they could use Stones
for wisdom, for healing, for manifesting what they really wanted.

All the learnings of all the ages live and breathe in your cells.
Call them out.
Let yourself be guided by the bounty of life all around you and deep within you.
It is all speaking with you.
Learn from those stories.
If you want awareness, choose it.
It will come and find you.
The more you choose it, the more it will find you,
it will create your life
it will hone your destiny.

If you forget that you have profound awareness within and all around,
place a piece of me to your third eye.
Wait until a dream of something-else-somewhere-else
lands upon you.
Whatever it is it has a gift of learning for you.
Open it because you are choosing awareness.

B

Basalt

I am a volcanic, igneous rock formed from magma near the Earth's surface. I am usually gray to black and very fine-grained due to rapid cooling. I have also been found on the Moon, Mars, Venus and the asteroid, Vesta. The oceanic tectonic plates are mostly composed of me, Basalt.

Emotional (Crystalline Grid) Bridge: Everything is made up of feelings here. We are breath and bone and most of all, feeling. Even its sediment literally sculpts every lifeform here. Reach your heart into that. Dive into the pure life of it.

Evolutionary Support: I am the exhale. I am the rainbow still forming behind the clouds. I am the renewal that you crave. My presence relaxes you even when you don't realize it. It softens your body which has stiffened to keep up with your unneeded expectations.

Tools for Co-Creation

I am the sigh after a big test.

I am the teeny green shoots that squeak out in your garden
after a long winter.

Put me on your desk, your nightstand, your altar.
I will remind you that after you get done
planning
measuring
predicting life,
life happens.
It colors inside AND outside of the lines.

I am relief if you let me be.

Carry me in your pocket and repeat,
"I am what I need to be."
"I do what I need to do."

Then just keep living.
Don't let the illusion of some unnecessary order
stop you from coloring, squeaking, sighing, and softening,
in any direction you choose.

Spill over the lines.

Bixbyite

I am a black mineral named for Maynard Bixby who originally found me in Utah. I am Manganese, Iron and Oxygen. I form in cubic crystals and have also been found in Sweden, Spain, South Africa, India and Argentina.

Emotional (Crystalline Grid) Bridge: Life is the invitation to open your heart and then to keep opening it, and then to open it more and bigger and brighter.....and then to keep opening it, in the face of more pain than you ever believed was possible.

Evolutionary Support: I ask everything to swirl and to circulate more freely. I love being held on your body so that every stiffness unknots. Your heart unlocks: You cry, you explode, you grin. You dance your feelings on the outside and your skin just shines.

Tools for Co-Creation

Got a blockage?
Put me there and exhale like a huge whale spouting ocean and air.

Keep doing it until freedom fills you
and overflows you.

Then
you will always have more energy and more talents to give and to be.

Take care of your body.
It speaks your mind.
It explores your dreams.
It cries your heart.
It walks your spirit,

Even if you don't believe it
or never noticed.

Personal Story

I have had the distinct honor to live with several black lingams for a couple years. Right after they became available I ordered as many as I could afford; one of which never had a specific place to be in the house. All the others had pots of sand to stand in and this very nice, medium sized stone just lay on it side waiting. Until one day my friend returned from a very stressful trip. That lingam quietly whispered, "Take me there."

So I did. My friend shared that she always wanted a Black Lingam but could not afford one. She just shared with me tonight that since I and the stone had been in her house, no one has entered without walking up to it and touching it. She feels that it has profoundly benefited her life and that of her autistic son. She senses that it calms the energy and slows things down to make things more palatable for him (and everyone).

One spoke for my husband and he sleeps next to it every night. I truly believe he would not be the man he is today without the stones in our home.

(con't on next page)

Black Lingams

Shiva Lingams were written about in "Stones Alive!, Volume 1." If you don't have that volume, this is what was said: "Like all true wonders, no two people can agree upon what exactly I am. You can locate me by the Narmada River, high in the Amandhata Mountains, which is one of seven sacred pilgrimage sites in India. It has been theorized that I was formed from a meteorite in the river bed millions of years ago. Most often, I am brown or gray combinations of chalcedony, agate and quartzite. My most distinguishing trait comes from deep red/maroon iron oxide markings."

The Narmada River has recently been dammed and much flooding has occurred from where these precious Stonebeings come. There is also supposedly talk of increasing significantly the height of the dam which would further increase the flooding of this area. Not having been to the area personally, it is challenging to filter through the different versions we hear of this information, including the possibility of no longer being able to access this region and these Stonebeings because of the flooding.

We were personally in the Himalayas in Nepal, and in every single temple we visited that contained a Shiva Lingam, that Lingam was full black in color. How interesting that we would rarely ever encounter a full, black Shiva in this country. Now is the time.

Please read the Stonestory included here for more about what the Black Shivas say about themselves.

Emotional (Crystalline Grid) Bridge: Yes. We bridge you to the Crystalline Grid, because that is our love. There will be no mental understanding of it, yet you can experience it if you choose it. You can go to the Grid through every feeling in every cell and it is your reality. It is your home. It is you, and it is us.

Evolutionary Support: This is the time to evolve. Everything that we have ever seemed to be arises within us now, strong, straight and free. This lifestalk will create the new world— the one that births in peace and choice.

Touch us. Come with us to the pure Center of the Earth Mother. Our roots are there; they intermingle without judgment, without fear. Revel in our intertwined roots. Let their pulse enter your heart and beacon us to the new world.

Tools for Co-Creation

Hold us until you know our heart.
They pound within yours.
They rest inside your stillness and your passion.

It is time for us to fully join together.

Wherever we place ourselves with full presence,
we enter the Crystalline Grid.
It enters us.
The freedom seems almost unbearable.....
we must know it to choose the new way of
Peace.

We co-create it here
now.

I have seen profound growth and learning in him since he has engaged more consciously.

I realize that I too have been profoundly changed by the Shivas. I am able to identify and respectfully release so much in their presence as they compassionately insist that I let go of what no longer serves me. This is a tremendous gift of service from them. I feel my relationship to them change and evolve. Today, I seek to create a relationship with them that includes the benefit of the whole. Seeking to see with compassion and purpose each person that enters my life, to have clarity and discernment in my daily actions and to live an honest life. I seek to be more of who I really am and express it joyfully. This, for me, requires support and great trust, the Shivas provide this. Their quiet voice encourages my spirit every moment and only asks that I am willing to trust in return.

~Cari W.

Personal Story

I am the Grandfather Lingam, who lives next to the front trees. I am part of a joining of the Earth Mother and the humans that intertwined through time and space.

For humans, the Narmada River was honored as a place where creativity flowed and was honed by the holy people who lived nearby. That part of the Earth Mother is a direct channel to the core of her gifts and her generosity. It linked people to the Earth's heart and belly and all of her senses. Through the Stones that she issued forth from there, she showed humans how to always be able to go directly inside the Earth to the core, to the Temple of Existence.

Some of the shamans and holy people have done this through the Ages and this has made the Earth Mother receptive and kind to all people everywhere.

Now the River is changing. It is being used for other things than to give humans a direct link to the belly of the Earth Mother. The Lingams that carried that vibration will one day stop being born from this River and channel. So the ones that are already here are themselves coming together and offering a bridge from humans to the Earth Mother.

The geometries that we offer now are for all humans and all beings. The season of the shaman who made it possible for others to feel the depth of the Earth Mother is transforming. That journey and that link now invites all humans to be shamans of some kind and exactly in the place where they already are.

The River now must run inside of each human who will allow themselves to finally be at home upon the Earth. We Lingams will intensify that message and that bridge for awhile. Because of our unique Earth bodies, we can especially link humans easily, clearly and ever exponentially with the Crystalline Grid- first the Earth Mother's, and then their own still birthing inner Crystalline Grid.

My heart rings an eternal Om. That Om was issued forth from the deepest roots of the Earth Mother. That is my language. It is my way.

I will take on the human words that you long for from other Beings of life that share this home with you. By doing that I will grow, I will deepen my place within and all around the Crystalline Grid. My sharing of your language brings me many others.

Personal Story

A few years ago I had asked Marilyn for some stones for my cats. She sent the most amazing clear quartz lingam for my beloved cat, Puffer. I rolled it in a bandana and tied it around his middle. He wore it throughout the winter and most of the spring and fall. He said it helped his arthritis. At first I didn't know how that could be possible until one night I woke up in the middle of the night and Puffer was laying across my arm in such a way that the lingam was on my arm. I felt this incredible vibration and heat radiating out across my arm. No wonder he said it helped his arthritis!

~Allison A.

Today I also invite you to a language that innately speaks with and through me. Sound, as it is, is carried, stored and transmitted by Crystalline fibers. I know that you are used to your own devices that use Crystalline fibers, yet that is different. I am not here speaking your easiest language so that you can use me without considering it. Instead, I directly invite you to join me within a journey as deeply into the Earth Mother as you can go. Meet me there. I will find you at whatever depths you offer and assume. Let us Om there.

Before you read any further into these Stone heart stories, go into the Earth Mother kindly with full intent to honor the ways and the languages of all beings upon the Earth. Do not make any lack of understanding an excuse to disregard any others' vibrations, gifts or consciousness. Be fully aware in your journey. Turn your attention into full circles all around your body in all directions. Receive the pure creativity from the Earth Mother as shamans have done by the banks of the Narmada River.

I will Om with you, around you and through you on your journey and with this Earth alchemy you will transform yourself. You will awaken your cells. You will claim your birthright even though you have forgotten it. You will sharpen your senses and new languages will shape your body. Keep journeying until you already know.

Then I invite you to go back through these words I have just offered. As you take them in, Om with me. Let us speak the same languages at the same time. You will find that between the normal words laying upon these pages innocently I will speak directly to your new cells and your new rooting into the Earth Mother and your deeper consideration of all life. I will and am speaking a language that is uniquely Crystallized to you. The message will be there when you truly arrive.

Peace.

~Grandfather Lingam

Personal Story

Maybe my wife can work this out a little bit because I would like this to come out in an easy way so that the ideas flow. (Which she is doing.) Sometimes things are jumbled in my head and the process of living and sleeping near my Black Shiva Lingam has brought me some clarity in ways I had not realized until recently. The stone came to me through my wife's listening. Originally, when she asked me if I wanted it I said, "No, I am okay." Turns out she ordered it anyway and it just lived with us. Each night she watched me curl up next to that stone on the living room floor or bench press it while watching television. The relationship was there, being established first by my spirit and then much later by my conscious awareness, only then could I feel the Lingam and the effect of it on my life. It's "tricky" (the Lingam), I only realize now what's been happening all along.

Sleeping next to this Shiva, it eventually made its way to my side of the bed and is sitting upright in a beautiful teal glazed pot and it has continued to bring up experiences in my dreams that can be disturbing. I often don't like how I feel or understand why the images are happening. At one point, I think I might have been mad at this stone if I had realized it was a catalyst for all of this discomfort. I would carry my dream experience through my day. Often times they were feelings I didn't like. I realize now these things are designed as tests. In other words, the Shiva has brought to the surface unresolved addictions, feelings and habits I need to re-evaluate and make current decisions about. I'd like to get this right. This is a process in which I can FEEL what is happening but I can't explain it very well.

I believe that the Shiva has taught me about clarity and truth. I have had a habit of defining myself as totally laid back about everything and I have learned that this is not true. There are things I do feel strongly about and when I don't take a stand for those things or make a clear commitment, I create a vicious cycle of inner-dialogue saying," No, that doesn't bother me. Wait! Yes it does, no it doesn't, Arrrgh, yes it does," and the tension then builds. I would get angry at my life, my job, or my wife, in order to vent that tension and I realize now, that is not what I want.

The Shiva has ultimately taught me that I DO have a unique hearts desire. There are things I AM passionate about and I have the inner drive to get clear about what really matters to me. I have also learned that there are two kinds of power, false and authentic. For a long time, what drove me was to attain: material things, a good job, or a relationship to give me a sense of identity. This lets you down though because it is false power. I have also learned to recognize it in other people too. I see guys in positions of power who can't be respected or they just don't have it for themselves. So I have learned about authenticity too, what is real and what isn't. True or authentic power has to do with people respecting you naturally because of

Personal Story

Shiva Lingams have been a profound gift for me since my fist meeting with two of them in Marilyn and Tohmas' room at the Tucson Gem and Mineral Show in 2004. In that first encounter, I was very attracted to one of them and quite afraid of the other. As I shared my feelings with Marilyn and Tohmas, they offered that the one I "liked" had strong feminine energy, while the other was more masculine. I got that the invitation was for me to connect more deeply with the masculine parts of my self that frightened me, and so I brought that lingam home, and began a relationship with these sacred beings that has supported my healing immensely ever since.

For me, they offer a constant invitation to not only connect with the sacred center of my being, but also to co-create each moment and event of my life as a choice to be present, to be listening and to be myself.

In my life now, I embody this in my daily practice of massaging each of the lingams here with oil every morning,

(con't on next page)

how you operate or the sense you get from accomplishing what it is you set out to do while being clear about your real hearts desire. I have learned that it has less to do with other people's opinions and more to do with my own. I have learned where I have been fooled and how I have seen others fooled by material desires or addictions.

I know that I have many things to learn. The thing is, the Lingam by my bed has helped me realize the need for clarity and authenticity in my life. I am not a passive person and there are things I deeply care about. I have a strong mind and spirit and need to live in alignment with them. This process can be hard because so much comes up to heal and resolve. I have made a lot of decisions in my life for the "wrong" reasons. In order to get where I choose to go I need to revisit those decisions and belief systems and choose again. I know I have opposition to some of these energies and emotions as they surface but now choose to be free of my anger and the drama that comes along with it. It's clear that acceptance and love need to enter in as I move through these experiences and choose a new perspective. Also, I choose to heal my cynicism and judgment of others, no matter where they are.

I think this story could be true for a lot of people. It seems there's a lot of us trying to grow or grow-up. Ultimately, my relationship with the Shiva is teaching me how to make decisions about what is most important in my life and what kind of energies and vibrations I want to entertain and have around me. It is very important that I learn to discern my own true vibration- who I am. I have been a part of a lot of other people's energies and experiences, now I choose to find out what is mine and really feel it easily and with joy.

So in learning about false power and authenticity I have become more clear and in tune with the fact I am not a passive observer in life. I care about things and choose to live my life knowing what those things are and what they are not. I choose to spend time listening to my heart and discerning its unique voice and living my life to honor it.

With the help of my dreams and the Black Shiva Lingam, I do know this so far: my heart's desire is I am a man who is very steady, stable and true. I am growing up to become him.

~Andy W.

at their invitation. Within this ritual I feel my breathing slow and deepen, flowing from toes to crown and calling together all the scattered parts of myself. Then there is an opening along the front of my body as my defenses melt, and I release the need to close myself off and hold myself back. I bask in and am held by the infinite love and support of the Earth Mother as embodied in the stone. From this place, I can listen and receive the wisdom that is offered to me, and then carry it into my day.

I also have a pocket-sized lingam I often carry with me or hold, and this supports me in re-membering that it's safe to be in my body, to be present with what's going on and to express myself.

These stones are a precious gift in my life for which I'm endlessly grateful.

~Lynn A.

Personal Story

My grandson was due to arrive on Earth June 14th, 2005, but as angels due they surprise us sometimes and he chose to start his entry earlier then that. My daughter Rita and I went to visit Tohmas and Marilyn during the Gem and Mineral Show here in Tucson in February and as soon as Rita arrived in the room she sat down on a large green Shiva Lingam gracing the center of the room. She just sat there for the longest time with her belly full of our angel and rested while I moved through the room and spoke with many of the crystals and stones on the shelves. At one point Marilyn sat next to Rita and asked if she could speak with the angel Rita was carrying, of course Rita gave her permission. Marilyn shared that he was healthy and happy to becoming to live with us, that all was well. She did not share that Kai told her he wanted to come early. Marilyn gifted Rita a small black Lingam to take home for him once he landed on Earth.

The day after Easter we went to the normal six month check up at the doctors and they told Rita she was in labor. Understand Rita deals with massive amounts of back pain daily due to a RSD condition so she is used to pain and did not realize the extra pain was actually labor pains. She was rushed to the emergency room and for the next month she laid in a hospital room not allowed to get up because her cervix had dissolved and there was nothing left to stitch up to help hold the baby in her uterus.

Kai Marley Nelson arrived on April 14th, 2005 a healthy baby boy even though he came two months early. Rita did an amazing job during delivery and I kept chilled stones on her back and legs throughout the full experience. The nurses and doctor were amazed at how comforting the cold stones were for her and were pleased that I was there to assist them for Rita was not allowed the normal medications they would give most women during delivery due to her RSD condition (a small blessing actually).

Once the medical team got Kai situated and in his little glass box I asked if we could put some personal items in with him; they said it was okay. Rita and I placed the black Shiva Lingam that Marilyn had gifted her in February, an angel card and a Jade stone. One nurse said that we might want to rethink that because they are not responsible for items missing. I said no worries, these items won't go anywhere, and of course they didn't. There are no fascinating stories to tell about the stones in Kai glass bed other then to say that most people did not even see them and the few that did were shy in asking what they meant to us. Kai came home five weeks

Personal Story

Certain stones are choosing to be with me at this time in my life. My emotional response to a stone is their way of making their connection known to me. A couple of months ago, I met a Lingam and I saw its swirling energy and called it the Hummingbird Lingam, as if I instantly knew its gift. It had an unusual green color along with the distinct gray, red and maroon markings of a Lingam. I thought of the Costa's Hummingbird. I have not been able to forget it. I felt that it was continuing to speak to me from another city and asking to be here on the land, in the desert, where I live. I am trusting what is being offered and saying, "Yes," accepting the responsibility that comes with being in a relationship with this stone being.

Today, it is arriving and I am excited.

~Eleanor S.

later and the black Shiva still sleeps in his room with him. While he was an infant we kept it in his bed but now that he is everywhere on the bed it rests on his shelf near his bed and guards his dreams for him.

Shortly after the birth of Kai, Tohmas came to our home for a LaStone session with me and he gifted me two of the most beautiful green Shiva Lingams that were perfectly energetically matched as well as physically partnered with one another and fit in the palm of my two hands nicely. Of course these beauties joined us on our Stone Walk that afternoon and later accompanied me to bed that night to meet me in my dreams.

As the days rolled by and the Shiva Lingams joined me in my Stone Walk each day my clients always asked the same question, "what kind of stone is this," when they were placed in their hands for the very first time.

None of my clients in those first few months knew what a Shiva Lingam stone was, but they all knew there was something different about them and it was not their shape that drew them to want to know more; it was the energy, the vibration they offered to the clients. They knew upon touching them something was different and these stones held a vibration that awakened something deep within their souls.

As time kept moving and my teaching expanding with the mineral kingdom, my students also wanted to incorporate the healing energies of the Shiva Lingam Stones in their practice. I personally use them for hand stones and one behind the neck for a pillow. I found that this triangle of energy that they create aids in balancing the Chakras. I have a smaller one that I rest in the center of my fish stone that I place on the Solar Plexus and Spleen Chakras. With this Shiva pointing upward and the other three creating the triangle or Trinity there is a powerful serge that flows through the client's body and support us both on the journey we are about to take with the mineral kingdom and the seasons through the touch of temperatures seeping deep into their bodies.

I also found that the Lingam stones hold heat better then any other stone I have in my set; even the darkest of the basalt stones can not hold the heat as long as the lingam stones do and they also love to roll over the muscles of the clients and be held in a sacred place on the body as I work with other stones and crystals throughout a session.

Time continues to move and one day a student of mine fell in love with the two green Shiva Lingams that Tohmas had gifted me in 2005. As the days flew by in the workshop I knew I would be releasing these green beauties to this woman and had to take them to bed each night to be sure my heart was in the right place for them to find a new home and someone else to walk with them. On the last day of the course I was ready both emotionally and spiritually to gift them freely without attachment to this woman and in so doing she was moved to a space of gratitude that she had not felt in years. No one had ever gifted her such a magnificent present before and it was hard for her to receive my offering without us going through a transition process that it is her birth right to be gifted beauty and love in this life time. All the students in that class room had insight into their own challenges with accepting a gift without the need to feel they owe you something in return. That closing day was actually the beginning of a new life for each of us as we walked away knowing we are all worthy of being gifted abundance and love everyday of our lives.

In 2007 Tohmas and Marilyn both came for stone sessions with me and they brought with them a large black Shiva Lingam that wanted to come and live with us. Kai fell in love with this black beauty right away. Shiva now stands below my massage table in a bed of sand that Kai keeps changing with his fingers now and then.

After the Gem Show in 2008 Tohmas and Marilyn asked if I would allow them to place four large Shiva Lingams in our back yard for safe keeping. Of course we were delighted and excited for these stones to join our land and help us hold and bring balance to our lives at this time. It was an exciting day for all but mostly for Kai, because a big Semi flat bed truck came to his house with a big crane and lowered "Tohmas and Marilyn's Shiva's in his yard" as he tells people who stop by to feel the energies of these enormous stone beings.

On the day the Shiva stones arrived in the backyard it was mid February and Baby-T (the 85 pound turtle in the picture) was still hibernating. He woke up before we got the Shiva stones in place and now he likes to nestle down between them, sometimes he gets stuck and I need help getting him out. Like in this photograph we needed our neighbor's help to pick him up and over the Shiva stones. You can not move the stones, they weigh thousands of pounds and Baby-T is about 2.5 feet long and weighs only about 85 pounds.

Like whales swimming in the ocean, these Lingams move energies in and around our home, they spiritually join me when I offer stone sessions in my office, they follow me in my dreams and they spin our property with vibrations that calls out to the wild animals in the area. Lately we have a couple of Quail nesting in our yard over the South African turtle's house. How they chose a yard with three large dogs and turtles to raise their young only demonstrates that the Shiva Lingams are balancing out nature and supporting all to survive equally together in harmony and respect for one another.

~Mary Nelson, founder of LaStone Therapy®

Personal Story

I am the Grandfather Lingam. (I am 4 millions years old only, by my own reckoning. I am still very young upon the Earth Mother.) Like all other Lingams, I stretched out and reached a peak of energy. For now, our numbers are limited and therefore, very precious. So we will focus who and what we are. We are a gift to be given without abandon to all the two-leggeds because their need is strong.

They too have reached a peak. The energy that they have offered the learning of separation has come to a point. This point is sharp and allows them to realize they can choose anything. They can choose separation. They can choose union. They can choose anything. This is always been so.

Yet why is the message so accelerated now?

We Lingams join our energy as never quite before. In the past Ages of humans, we have mostly held the space for rooting the third eye into all things. We have mostly spoken with and from the Eastern part of the Earth Mother, where they allowed and nurtured the journey of Spirit and Reality. So we represented that ever growing creativity. We nurtured it with all our being.

During the seeming passage of time, we have watched the humans change. They dance like Dervishes in their constant transformation of being. They have grown their creativity profoundly, but they have not always interwoven it with their Spirit. That is why we also have come to the West, just as many other ways and words of Spirit have come now. It is the season to marry what seems to be opposite- East and West, Earth and Sky, Spirit and everyday human reality, and so on.

We Lingams speak for now. I do not speak for myself alone because it is not possible. I am joined with all others. It is simply that we who are of the largest sizes gather the most attention from humans. So I stand up and I speak as clearly as all my ancientness allows, perhaps even demands.

Welcome human children of the Earth Mother. Please come beside me now. I have been born and grown for this moment. I speak for the fullness of being to your hearts. That is why we can come together across time and space and still see and hear and feel each other as if we were physically touching hands.

Join me in the Crystalline Grid. You do regardless. Yet, if I give you this invitation out loud in your own words, then the parts of you that have felt so hurt by not feeling, by not belonging with everything on the Earth, they can at least begin to hear me, to feel warmth after a bone-chilling cold.

Join me in the Grid. It is our home. It is our togetherness.

I came into a body so that I could invite you ALL to be in and with the Crystalline Grid. You humans have such a beautifully unique journey. You pretend to be separate from all of us while all the rest of us children upon the Earth Mother are linked. We know this. It is not in our destiny to be able to pretend that we are separate, even if we want to.

You pretend the separation with such a fierceness that you now draw me to you to say just as potently, we belong together. Our cores live in the Grid. That is where we know all, and all forgetting and all illusions drop away and become seeds for other remarkable journeys elsewhere.

You are SO ready to hear this. It is the eve of your birthing your own evolution. You can pretend to deny hearing me and believing what I bring to you. But it does not matter. Now those pretenses are old voices that you are exorcising and I am witnessing for and with the Grid. You can protest, but we are joined.

The Earth Mother was and is created by Spirit. For some, you will recognize that as the central Sun of this Universe. However we now speak this, it is true. She was and is continually formed as a raw development of feeling. As we watch her turn and marvel at the Sun, we see she is too young, growing, maybe even immature, when stood next to other members of this Universe. It does not matter. What is important is that she is given to express all heart into form. She does it without judging or even what you would call sense or logic. Because of this, it attracts multitudes of beings who wish to experience a new realm that is almost all emotion.

Many came here to live with so much heart. The Crystalline Grid was formed as the core of that heart of the Earth Mother. It was placed into form so that she and the others upon her could experience the fullest spectrum of feeling possible- which does seem to humans to translate into polarities: limits and unlimitedness, lack and abundance, violence and peace.

The Grid was fully intended so that there would be unlimited choices for whomever landed upon the Earth Mother. The Crystalline Grid is electrical lifeforce that has crystallized and condensed into solid-ness. In this form, magnetics and electricity join and that is the foundation of the Earth Mother and therefore of life here. The Grid communicates her heart instantaneously, to herself, and simultaneously, projects it to all directions and all beings. Every beat of her heart right now echoes in every human, every plant, every animal, every feeling. And perhaps most especially, every Stone.

Each Mineral upon this planet carries a piece of the Crystalline Grid. It is undeniable. It is what composes their cells. Wherever they land, they infallibly hear and speak the heart of the Earth Mother. Do you know what her heart asks of them?

Remember, she was/is designed as an oasis for emotions, for breeding feelings. It is her service in this Universe. She does it in her own flowering uniqueness. Because it is unusual and even somewhat new, she asks the core of her being, the Grid and the resulting Crystals, to record every experience and every single emotion, to and from forever.

That is the service, even the duty, of every Stone.

They live without judgment so they can simply record all. So while they are surrounded by great passion, they must also remain free and utterly detached. The Crystalline Grid connects all Stones so that they will always in all of their witnessing still remain clear, free. They are the Sacred Witnesses of the Earth Mother for this Universe.

Their stories speak to the Earth of her development, of her generous choices. They offer the same to all the children upon her, simultaneously; they beam their communications into Space so that the gift and the challenge of living in your heart would be shared with ANY who wished to accept the invitation in any way.

Some beings come from far away to live here. Some stay upon their own Stars and their own learnings, yet they listen to the Crystalline Grid and they explore emotion from there. If humans knew how many shadow their every step, they would be amazed, maybe a little afraid, too.

The Grid is the core blueprint for all life forms. If you choose to inhabit here you must wear a body that has been designed by the Grid that allows you to live with a focus of feeling. The Grid has designed four Elementals that extend outward into the four directions of the Earth's body. Basically, the Northeastern direction is Earth Elemental. The Southeastern direction is Water Elemental. The Northwestern direction primarily is imprinted by the Air Elemental. The Southwestern direction is imprinted by the Fire Elemental.

There are many, many other specific Elemental Imprints that have evolved to specific areas of the Earth. These are just the most basic gifts from the Grid. Humans traveling all over the Earth have helped all these areas to grow their own relationship with the Elementals. The Elementals are the INTENT of all form. They land in body and make up endless, perfect combinations of Fire and Earth and Air and Water.

The Ethers Elemental is where everything is connected and then the Earth is connected to all else, simultaneously.

The Grid with its Elemental Core, breeds geometries of life that can be seen as the common root of all life forms. All plants, animals and minerals, are Crystalline Beings. When you treat them as such, and speak to and listen to their hearts, they will create beyond the Grid.

That is where I come in now. I am one of many large Lingams who have felt the rising electricity and magnetics in the Grid. We know this is a wave of new creation. If we measure through time, and that is part of what we Crystals do, then we see that this wave is different. It is a new pattern of life. It comes from a new intent. All the Ages of the Earth have been imprinted and born of her desire to be a space of heart where others could join her at the point of their own freedom. She has lived and learned and flowed this, and now, to translate this into human words, the story says that she is growing, she is transforming, and she is extending her gifts into this Universe. She is no longer focused so much on her body and her children. She opens up her heart to give and receive the gifts of everything else as well.

I feel this. I know it is so. The Grid is translating as rapidly as possible. It is transmuting so that it is beaming its imprints and records all across the Earth and into Space simultaneously.

We large Lingams are the focus of those new, outward communications. We root so deeply into the Earth and we grow such acceptance that we are allowed to shoot out the stories of the Earth and her children to our Star families.

Perhaps it is not so unusual.

Perhaps it is the next journey and is inevitable.

Perhaps it is our constant evolution.

Yet, for humans, it is dramatic or it will FEEL so at times.

In order to communicate our heart with others, some of whom are wiser or stronger, we must be clear. We must be joined. All the children of the Earth Mother are being invited to come together and to admit to ONE HEART.

If, and as, the humans do this now, they will bring such power and such different stories to the Crystalline Grid. It is not that their stories are not already living there. It is that the feeling of their willingness and union does not quite yet breathe there. That seems to be the key. All feelings are here and have been dutifully recorded, even the shadow ones that the humans have offered.

All children upon the Earth Mother come together now to support the humans who will add their own unique acceptance to the Grid.

~Grandfather Lingam

Brazilianite

I was named after my first discovery in Brazil. My color ranges from colorless through greenish yellow to yellow. I can occur as well-formed crystals of precious stone quality and also as spherical aggregates. I sometimes occur on Muscovite and have also been found in New Hampshire, USA.

Emotional (Crystalline Grid) Bridge: I flash with such almost unbelievable brilliance. I do it with my body over ages. You do it with many bodies over many lives— the same, glorious radiance in unlimited ways and times. I am sighing now with your sweet heart.

Evolutionary Support: Touch me. Do you recognize me? I help people to relate to water, the most prevalent element on this planet. Ahhhhhhhh~

Water might seem common to you, yet it is still a miracle— unique in each droplet. I know this. I find the place in your heart where you know this. I stretch your wonder until it touches everything, everyone, all the time— including yourself.

Tools for Co-Creation

Sit down.
Go soft
while your spine stretches out
infinitely kindly.
Once it finds a safe, sweet spot that allows unhindered breath
close your eyes.

Open your third eye.

Truly revel in the world.
Gaze upon the energy
that pulsates alongside every form.

Hear my voice
while you watch the geometries of life swirl.

What do you see when you hear and feel me?
What colors do I wear?
The energy dance of my being touches yours.
What does that look like?

Take your time.
Take all time. Life loves sharing its wonders.
Drink in as much as you can.
When you are full,
open all of your eyes at once.

You are awake to the world.

Bytownite

I was first described in 1835 and named after an occurrence at Bytown, Ontario, Canada. I am a Calcium-rich mineral and form triclinic crystals, common twinning and fine striations. I can be grey to white to yellow and even brown or blue. I am Plagioclase Feldspar and have been found in Europe, Canada and Mexico.

Emotional (Crystalline Grid) Bridge: I am touching the inescapable wonder of you, maybe even more than you do! You are an adventurer, a discoverer! No one knows what you will find, what you will be—through time and space and beyond.

Evolutionary Support: Welcome! There are so many basic languages upon the Earth. There are feelings, sound, colors, movement....until eventually there are words, as well. I am very glad to be here in words for you, yet underneath those decorations, I give you

Purple

Warmth

Twirls

Flute echoes

Inside of those gifts, we are instantaneously ONE. That oneness clears your lungs, it sharpens your eyes and it digests your food.

Tools for Co-Creation

Keep me in a special jar that catches and twirls the light.
Only pull me out when you want to expand journeys of senses.

Put me by your nose when your favorite supper is cooking.
Put me in your hand when you hug your love after a hard day.
Put me by your ear when you are listening to a concert of a sweet CD.
Put me by your head before you go to sleep at night
so that you can remember your dreams.

Personal Story

I recently purchased a very nice lot of Mexican Bytownite, and along with it came one very large piece- large for Bytownite. It fits nicely in my hand and is easy to carry around. It is very translucent and a wonderful yellowish-greenish-clear.

I have had this piece near me since it came into my life and have made a point of always bringing it along on trips for some reason. So it was in my truck when I recently drove to Tucson for an appointment with our alternative dentist to have the mercury removed from my teeth.

This dental appointment was no small matter for me, having been appropriately tortured as a child by my then dentist (as so many of us have been). This layer though is only on the top of many other layers of fears created by years of alien abduction as a child. The whole dental office scene, as well as the tools used (especially the noises) can be terrifying for me. This dental scenario also includes a perpetual sense of giving away my lifeforce energy to an

(con't on next page)

I am here to focus, stretch, and swirl your senses.
Focus on me when you go on those journeys.

Personal Story

Even at our calmest, things are always rocking and rolling here at AhhhMuse (kind of like your life, right?), so when our computers don't work as needed, we start to feel the pressure mount pretty quickly. Luckily for us, we know a computer genius in town who can fix our technological difficulties in a flash, and he even does it calmly and with a smile.

Tom, our computer whiz, is a patient, bright man. He somehow manages to find time for all of it, even when he has no time. One day, I was picking up our hurting laptop and he chatted with me for a while, kindly showing me a few handy things about computers in the process.

Then he started talking about stones. Tom used to be in the quartz business somewhere in the Arkansas area, so he knew a bit about them. He was still into harvesting them, himself. When he would talk about rock hunting, he sounded like a little kid on a treasure hunt. You could tell that he loved getting outside and forgetting all about anything mechanical. He loved finding stones while he was amongst the trees and the peace of Mother Nature.

That day, he put some small, raw beige colored stones in my hand, "They're for you! Enjoy them." He was thrilled to give me a handful of his latest find. I know he said a lot more about them, but I just can't remember a single word. From the moment that the Bytownite touched my palm, they started talking, too.

They told me how they could soothe my nerves and help me remember that I am one being on a big, bright planet with plenty of "stars" on it. Through the heart of those Stonebeings, I swam with complete awe for this Earth. I could see it through their eyes and those eyes weren't missing a single color, a single sunrise—not even a single flash of sparkling quartz in the tar of the local highway. They whispered to me that everything is perfect and everything's always happening at the perfect time.

What a gift! Tom had given me something so wondrous, that I didn't really have any words for it. I was alive and I knew it, and that's how I left his shop that day.

outside authority, so I am also extremely sensitive to having others tell me what and/or how to live in my body and what to do with it. Exactly what a doctor always seems to do and I have been living my life for decades never accessing these people. I always choose to heal myself with the support of Spirit and the other kingdoms, Plant, Animal and Stone.

So I knew I would need help and the Bytownite raised its hand and I said, "Yes!" immediately I held the stone throughout my whole dental visit (they never mentioned it, even though they are very alternative and have many, many stones and crystals in the office) and it truly supported me in allowing ALL my feelings and emotions to arise and be accepted and then to move freely in them with a different definition than terror or struggle. I also found that the Bytownite had a unique capacity to not only incorporate and allow my current feelings but it coagulated feelings and experiences of many parallel lives, all happening at the same moment, for healing within this chosen dental experience, consciously.

(con't on next page)

A few weeks later, we had something come up with our computers that needed some help asap. Tohmas called Tom immediately of course. I asked him, "So can Tom get to this stuff right away?" And then when Tohmas didn't answer me right away, I said, "Oh, okay. He's not going to be able to get to it until later, right? He's held up by other things, isn't he?"

Tohmas said, "Yeah. He's not going to be able to get to it. He's dead. He just dropped dead last night."

I was momentarily stunned.

Then I felt the Bytownite that he had given us. I got it. I found the words, now. I knew that something in Tom knew that he was going to be leaving planet Earth soon, so before he left he wanted to pass on to us something of life—something that was bright and happy and vibrating with excitement. He wanted to share that with us while he still could.

I feel so honored by that. My heart just smiles. Every time I see any Bytownite, I laugh and say "Hi!" to Tom. I'm glad that the last time I saw him we shared life.

~Marilyn T.

So it is now an ever more trusted friend with an aware and conscious purpose that gets utilized in my life in an ever increasing fashion. Many thanks to this Bytownite and the Crystalline Grid for providing this deep and pure service and linking it to such a large, powerful and healing big picture.

~Tohmas T.

Cobaltite

I am Cobalt, Arsenic and Sulphur with smaller amounts of Iron and Nickel. Somewhat rare, I am mined as a source of Cobalt. My name is derived from the German, Kobold, which means underground spirit. I was found as early as 1832 in Cobalt, Ontario. I have been found in Europe, Canada, England, Australia, the Congo, and Morocco. I am reddish silver white to violet steel grey to black and form pseudocubic, granular to massive.

Emotional (Crystalline Grid) Bridge: E-a-s-e into yourself. If you rush into your body, it's going to jump! Be gracious with all of yourself. Ease into your heart and welcome yourself softly and gracefully.

Evolutionary Support: Relax.

I know you're "reading" now and your mind is switched on . . . but also . . . relax. That's where you'll find me. That's how you'll know my name. That's how you'll breathe in my gifts. In that relax , your body can nourish the unfed, unloved parts of you and welcome everyone home.

Tools for Co-Creation

You can work with me any way you like.

I go to the unique places within you that need
attention
that is particular
just to them.

I offer that attention
so that you can draw to you whatever

resources, circumstances, or feelings
will touch you
and remind you that you are well and loved.

You write here the ways that you want to co-create with me;
I will join you in a single relax.

Dolomite

I am usually massive and have properties similar to Calcite. I am Calcium Magnesium Carbonate $CaMg(CO3)2$ and am named for the French naturalist and geologist, Déodat Gratet de Dolomieu who first described me (supposedly) in the 1700's. My color is usually white, gray to pink. I can be found all around the planet and am common in Mexico and have famous exposures in the Alps in northern Italy. I am a soft mineral and have even appeared as growth in the kidneys of a dog. Recently, I have been located in highly saline environments, specifically in Australia and Brazil.

Emotional (Crystalline Grid) Bridge: Stillness.

All-that-is married to nothingness.

Join us.

Evolutionary Support: Peace comes in acceptance. With acceptance comes more. It breeds itself in cells that grow your body strong, rooted and simultaneously,

endlessly free.

I am in your bones. I am the bones of the Earth Mother. I accept this and she feels strong, rooted and simultaneously, endlessly free.

Tools for Co-Creation

I so love talking with you.
I am a storyteller
I keep all stories safe within my marrow
so that when you need one
it is ready—
ever ready for exactly the need you have
right now.

For every need
there is a story.

For every need
there already lives an answer.

When you ask to be filled with what you need
the answer already breathes within you
or you could not ask for it.
Its desire to immediately fulfill you
gives you inspiration to ask for it
and then to receive it
even if you don't know it or recognize it at first.

Don't you hear the answer?

When you ask the question—
strong,
rooted and simultaneously,
endlessly free—
listen
listen to the story that comes to you,
whatever it is
whatever it seems to be about
whether you understand just yet or not.
Listen: the questions and answers always meet
for you
in the Stonestories.

Listen with your bones.

Personal Story

Calcite has always been one of my favorites, and this one seems to be the most special of all for me. These golden-to-honey dogtooth crystals, or "stellar beams," have a very transcendental energy to them. They help ground me when teaching and seem to convey a very wise energy all their own.

The beautiful points of Pugh Calcite exhibit one of several distinct "personalities." The oldest formation from this historic location is a deeper honey brown color. They are very intricate and often form many large points, with complex twins and parallel growth. They are truly multidimensional tools. These crystals always seem to choose guardians that are deeply in tune and want to help others.

The second grouping could be considered a younger formation; they are delicate looking druses of crystals in a medium khaki color. Upon close inspection they are as beautiful and complex as their larger and older counterparts.

(con't on next page)

Flint

I am a hard, cryptocrystalline form of Quartz, known as a variety of Chert. I am usually dark grey, black, green, white, or deep brown in color. I occur mostly as masses and nodules in sedimentary rock formations such as Limestone or Chalk. It is not exactly clear how I form but one theory is that holes bored by crustaceans fill with a sediment that then becomes silicified. I have been used to make tools throughout the history of humankind.

Emotional (Crystalline Grid) Bridge: I am with you. Look where you don't expect to find any support: that's where I am. I land upon your world, quietly, but I can speak up LOUDLY when you need to feel that you are not alone.

Evolutionary Support: I can grow sharp edges. So can you. They point us toward our next steps up the hardest mountains.

I speak to you now so that you will feel my jaggedness, my strength, my beauty—all. Perhaps on this Earth, to be strongly yourself, you must jump into full-out initiation— maybe every day, maybe every moment. If this is so, feel that power pound within me, so that you can find it in you, too. Celebrate every challenge, if you want to be an unbelievably powerful treasure.

Tools for Co-Creation

Write down every hard thing you must do.
List them clearly, simply.
Feel your resistance rise up.
Feel your excitement pound, too.

Place a piece of Flint on top of the list.
With all your being

The third group is younger still. They are transparent, golden points in a very classic scalenohedron, or dogtooth shape. Some are double terminated, but all are luminous. These seem to zing with energy. They are really alive.

All the Pughs are special and sacred in my work. I love to share them wherever I go, and they generate attention only when they want to.

~Nick P.

ask for grace to be able to do everything
you must do and want to do
in spite of your doubts
in spite of anything.

Now go to bed
asking for grace
as you fall asleep.

When you wake up,
immediately do the most difficult thing on your list.

As you do it
you will feel the grace flow over you
caressing your hard edges.

Franklinite

I am part of the Spinel group of minerals. I was named after Benjamin Franklin and was originally found in New Jersey. I am a Zinc-rich, usually black, crystal with a specific octahedral shape.

Emotional (Crystalline Grid) Bridge: When you plunge into your heart to meet me, I will come any way you really wish. I will chant. I will hum. I will praise vociferously and I will comfort. Anything is possible. Everything is possible. Everything and anything are Now.

Evolutionary Support: Yes! Let me give you energy to use and to enjoy. It is who I am and what I have to offer and I do it with all my being and with all my heart.

I will fill your well. Drink from my energy and from my pure focus on being (and being with) pure lifeforce.

Tools for Co-Creation

I treasure life. It brings so many gifts.
I vibrate with its endless current.

When you feel tired, place me next to a glass of water, in the sunlight.
Ask me to fill the water with unlimited vitality.
Then drink it with great intent and acceptance.

You will feel my energy and the water refreshing every part of your being.

Fullerite

I am named for the free thinking inventor/architect/visionary, Buckminster Fuller, who invented the geodesic dome which illustrates the molecular morphology of Fullerenes. I can be found in Precambrian metamorphic rocks, interstellar space, lightning strikes on high carbon substrates, and metamorphism of carbon rich rocks. I have been found in Russia in sediments derived from meteor impacts called Shungites. I am also called Bucky Balls.

I am the solid-state manifestation of Fullerenes. Polymerized single walled nanotubes (P-SWNT) are a class of Fullerites and are compared to Diamond in hardness. However, the nanotubes do not have the same growth patterns as Diamonds and are not neatly and easily cuttable. This same growth pattern though results in a stronger material. Nanotubes are very expensive to produce in quantity so they have not replaced steel or similar materials in our common usages. Ultra-hard Fullerites, Buckyballs, are a form of carbon synthesized under high pressure and high temperature. It is believed that Fullerene is three-dimensionally polymerized in this material and its hardness is a complex and controversial issue. It was originally claimed that it was harder than Diamond but these claims have not been confirmed somehow. This is complicated by poor crystallinity of the samples due to the high pressures involved in producing superhard materials. The hardest samples were reported to be amorphous and "most likely with most of the fullerene cages collapsed into diamond-like carbon phase." This material has also been used to create an even harder material called, Aggregated Diamond Nanorods.

In my carbon form I look much the same as what you are used to seeing as the structure of a geodesic dome. In mathematical terms, "the structure of a fullerene is a trivalent convex polyhedron with pentagonal and hexagonal faces."

Minute forms of me are found in nature as soot and also are formed by lightning discharges in the atmosphere. As Fullerite, I am a molecule composed entirely of Carbon, am black or grey and very brittle.

Emotional (Crystalline Grid) Bridge: When you are separate from your Spirit and from All-That-Is, you feel alone. In that loneliness you never know that you are awesomely talented and that you can handle anything you choose.

I offer you the energy of being perfect for everything in your life. Accept it. Please. Whenever anything startles you, I give you the underlying certainty, "I can do this!"

Evolutionary Support: There are so many inspirations continually swirling in the Ethers just waiting for you to see them and to love them. Look at them! There are as many of them as snowflakes in a blizzard. They are as omnipresent as air. I will point them out to you, forever, and I love each one.

Tools for Co-Creation

Make a list of everything that you really love.
Talk about every part of your delight.

Make a list of everything that you do well.
Spare no details about any of your talents (This list is just for your eyes!!! So go for it!).

Savor these lists.
Let their joy carry you through every struggle.
After you have read them so constantly that you have memorized them,
combine them.
Marry the talents that you have to the joy that you love.
Let them come together, every moment— in every act you can offer life.

I will always point out more inspirations~

G

Gem Silica

I am typically Chrysocolla in/with Quartz. I am usually a very high grade of Chrysocolla but I can have other copper occurring minerals included occasionally in my presentation. I am a very uniform color of blue and have been found in Arizona, Peru and South Africa as well as other places where copper occurring minerals are found.

Emotional (Crystalline Grid) Bridge: Here, take my overflowing heart. It spills over with sweet awe for you. As it spills, it warms your loneliness and it feeds all the flowers of the Earth's garden.

Evolutionary Support:

If you knew yourself, as I know you, you would never stop smiling! The whole Universe dances wild and free, within you. You shake— you threaten— and in the same breath, the tenderest Spirit stands over you, infinitely tall and regal.

Whatever you dream, you are. If you yearn for love, it melts within you or you could not imagine its preciousness. If you crave strength and freedom and riches, look within your heart, it already lives there in vaster realms than you can measure. Grasp every dream; its roots are in your body now. Grow them.

Tools for Co-Creation

I follow you!!

The creativity that explodes from you lights the world.

Survey its every spark.
You are here to be the artist of your life.

Dream bigger, stronger and even more foolishly.

Your life is an epic adventure even when it is a single, soft
Breath.

Glacial Etched Quartz

I am specifically, in this book, from the very high altitudes of the Pakistan mountains by K2 (although there is also a find in India). I am Quartz and my surfaces are etched by the movement of the mountain and by glaciers and I have been recently exposed through Global warming. (This is my story I am telling here, it does not necessarily come from a scientist or anyone else.). I come to you with my heart exposed in a time of great need. You can decide for yourself what I truly am if any else's explanations do not satisfy you. I remain myself.

Emotional (Crystalline Grid) Bridge: The coolness in me lands warmly upon you. Where the Earth Mother is high and clear, she speaks to all of us— Stone and Plant and Animal alike— freely and easily. The air may be stretched and thin where I come from, but the love is endlessly wide.

Evolutionary Support: Peace. I bring you peace. Please, please welcome it. When you do, see where it lands in your body and what it then urges you to do. Do what peace asks of you freely and you will free even more peace within you. It is so.

Tools for Co-Creation

Hold me willingly in your outstretched palm.
Now cup your other palm gently over me.
Slowly and smoothly press your palms together

Personal Story

We love meeting new Stones. They speak to us right away. They tell us their stories and they freely give us wisdom that we don't know if we could find any other way. They turn our heads . . . in more ways than one.

What's also amazing is when the Stones find us through truly amazing humans, as well. The Glacial Etched Quartz found us through such respectful, new friends, it made everything just flow: The Quartz glows with aliveness, with purity. It refreshes us so thoroughly that all our cells dance after handling just one piece. On top of that, it comes through humans who honor us and make us feel happier in life, too.

It dawned on us that this is not a coincidence. This Glacial Quartz comes from very high up in the Pakistani Mountains, and it has not been readily available before now. With all the turmoil and changes in that part of the world, we feel that one of the side effects of the human violence and struggle there is that the Stones are coming off the mountains and landing in

(con't on next page)

until you are embracing me like a tight, friendly hug!
Gently rub your palms over me for a full, intentional minute.
As you can, think of nothing as you do this.
Simply be alive.
Simply receive whatever comes to you.
Let go of the control of loneliness and struggle.

Feel the purity of my electricity meeting your electricity.
Now we can talk!
Now we can work and play and breathe together.
Do this as many times as you can every day.
Let our meetings shift and transform as they will.
Each time, you will free yourself to learn something so preposterously new that you will usher in unlimited lifeforce.

I won't tell you what we will talk about or what we will do then.
I will simply await your touch.
I am here.

the hands of the humans who truly need them.

When we listened with the Stonebeings, they told us that the Middle East, and areas near that, help through the Elementals to release so much dramatic emotional energy from all over the world. It is a profound, sacred service that the Stones in those areas offer all of us. So while we, humans, sometimes, fill those lands with our pain, the Stones and Crystals in turn fill us with the most clarifying, exponential love. They help us where and how we most need it.

Can you feel it? The unconditional love and pure support of the Stones are filling us right now.

~Marilyn and Tohmas T.

Glauberite

I am Sodium Calcium Sulfate. I am soft, tabular and brittle. I can also be found as bladed aggregates. I am similar to Selenite/Gypsum and am clear to grayish. I am named after Glauber's Salts, an alchemical product. I can be found in Europe, India, Russia and the USA, among other places. I am often associated with salt beds and fumeroles- cavities linked to dormant volcanoes.

Emotional (Crystalline Grid) Bridge: PLAY! Roll in the dirt and I will cover you with enough awe and glory to last through anything. Somersault downhill and dance uphill. Climb the trees and yodel. I will answer. I am answering you right now: I am with you whenever you delight in the sheer ecstasy of loving your ever-perfect life. It fits you!!

Evolutionary Support: Every day you learn something. Every moment life brings you a precious gift. Bit by bit the learnings and the gifts shape you, as a human sculpture. They will carve your bones and flow your blood.

With me, you can look at your form— see what vastness it can tell you about life. Together, we will read your body as the book it is— that knows all your choices and all your possibilities.

When you hold me, you will remember consciousness......

Tools for Co-Creation

Peace my friend.
I know that it can be scary or strange listening to a Stonebeing.

However,
whenever
you want to listen with me (or not)
I am here.

I am as ancient as the winds.
I am as timeless as the sky holding the earth.
That is who I am and it is what I offer,
freely.

I don't expect you to be anything except what you are
or what you choose to freely give me.

I will wait forever to know you.
It is the way of the Stones and of unlimited wisdom.
Come to me by any dream or fancy that catches your heart.

Whenever you want to be with me,
it is already so.

Personal Story

Glacial Etched Quartz

This quartz has been a sacred addition to my journey. This mineral always feels so quiet and reverent. Whenever I am in need of true and utter stillness, I just have to ask it to co-create with me. This is one of the newer crystalline allies that seems to be grabbing the attention of humanity in very subtle ways. These emerging crystals don't have to be big and loud to jump out at us, but they are tender and sweet. Their vibrations reach us at the core.

The Pakistani Ice crystal that I have gotten to know feels like it is carrying a message of looking deep within to help us read what is written in our souls. Just like the etched surfaces of these sacred stones, we are whole unto our divine selves, full of all the connections to Spirit and the answers to life's mysteries. Our potential might lay hidden beneath a glacier, but even glaciers and mountains can be moved by Spirit's might. We just have to listen. This crystal has reached out to many of my own students, and it seems to instill a certain quiet knowing in each of us.

~Nick P.

Goethite

I was named after the German, Johann Wolfgang von Goethe, and am an iron bearing oxide mineral found in low temperature environments. I have been used as a paint pigment throughout history and my first described occurrence was on the Mesabi Iron Range of northern Minnesota in 1806. I can be yellow, to red, to dark brown and, in a sense, am iron ore. I tend to weather out of other iron rich minerals and so am a large component of some soils. Lepidochrosite is a polymorph of my Iron Oxyhydroxide.

Emotional (Crystalline Grid) Bridge: I SO love you. With all that I am, I know how fragile you can be in your deepest emotions. I sigh. You are enough. You are enough to outlast it all and you have always been this. You will always be this.

Evolutionary Support: I root you. I bring you right to this moment and to full breath. See the tremendous vista of life and the unlimited bounty that the Earth offers you, not just now, but every moment—every moment that you truly choose.

If you can, gaze into the vastness of everything when you act upon your wishes; this shapes your life into forever. It is not what you do that shapes you infinitely, it is how you do it.

Tools for Co-Creation

Place me next to you.
Meditate quietly until breath and temper are one.
In the void of simply being, awaken fully.
Open your eyes, bright, again.
Drink in all that is, just as it is.
Leave behind illusions forever.
They can only serve those who do not want to live.

Write down, or speak, one at a time, the major traumas scarring your being right now.
Give them full breath and endless consideration in just listening to their stories and in calling them out.
There is no need to say anything else, until you invite them to join you in the bright-awake world, instead of half-living in your shadows.

Give them the full light of your unjudging gaze.
See them as they are.
Simply see.

One by one, ask them to join into the fullness of you.
Combine talents.
As you accept each one, cradle me in your arms and say,
"I am whole. I am the vastness of the universe, alive and free."

Heulandite

I am a soft mineral of the Zeolite group. I have a pearly luster which can be orange, brown, red, yellow, or green. I was first distinguished from Stillbite by August Breithaupt in 1818. He called me, «Euzeolite,» (meaning beautiful Zeolite). Independently in 1822, H. J. Brooke arrived at the same result giving me the name Heulandite, after the mineral collector, Henry Heuland. I am most common in Iceland and India and have been found as beautiful yellow crystals near Baltimore, Maryland.

Emotional (Crystalline Grid) Bridge: Life is strong. It is stretching itself over itself, from impossibility to possibility in all directions.

Hold me to your heart now. You FEEL my words and you can co-create anything.

Evolutionary Support: I awaken the oldness in you that does not bring you life any more. I shake it up. Can you see the death you breed in your distractions and your resistances?

Tools for Co-Creation

Run me over your body, without actually touching you.
Feel your blood swirl.
Breathe into the places where you need to let go of pain or stagnation.
Do this as often as you can until you can just relax with my presence.
Now run me over your skin.
Let me touch your bumps, bruises and all your impatience.
I will vibrate them all.
Breathe into every one of them.
Give each soreness as much time and as much attention as it takes.

Personal Story

Having taught geology at the university level for many years such topics as crystal structure, lattice network, electron arrangement and bonding types are a part of everyday conversation. I think formal training is important but we should be careful not to get hung up on all the technical details. It is important to be flexible while learning; not to be so set in our ways that we can't allow new perspectives to enter our little world.

My philosophy is to retain past knowledge while exploring new ideas and concepts. For example, if we are willing to recognize there is more to our world than the traditional 3-dimensional space and linear time, then anything is possible when exploring the physical, emotional and psychic healing properties of minerals.

Only recently have I begun to explore minerals for their healing properties. For years I've seen minerals only in "black & white"; now I'm beginning to see them in all their glorious colors. I now have Ajoite

(con't on next page)

Just be with them completely.
Let every part of you say and do what it needs to
as safely and as respectfully as possible.

Hypersthene

My name is Greek and means, "over-strength." I am found in igneous and some metamorphic rocks as well as in some iron meteorites. I form a solid solution series with the minerals Enstatite and Ferrosilite. There is no iron in pure Enstatite, while pure Ferrosillite contains no Magnesium. I am the mineral when a significant amount of both elements are present. My chemical formula is (Mg,Fe)SiO3. My color is usually gray, brown or greenish and I have a pearly luster with sometimes brilliant schiller. I am often cut and polished as a gemstone.

Emotional (Crystalline Grid) Bridge: I am an old, old crone. I have seen so much and so much has seen me. When you delve into me, you lose mysteries and find yourself reflected in thousands of ways, journeys, struggles and constant learnings.

Evolutionary Support: I live beneath the surface. I live away from the shimmering of the sun. It is quiet here. The stillness lets me be all that I am completely .

When I am with you, I feel the totality of you. I especially feel the parts that you don't and I invite them back to the whole, gently. If they don't remember the way home, I call out to them by name.

Tools for Co-Creation

Every human has parts of themselves that they left behind when the pain of staying whole was impossible.
When you get traumatized and can't remember love, that stunned part of you breaks away. It stays in the distress, marking the injury, so that one day when you are strong enough the full power of you will go back there and make everything one again.

and Chrysoprase at the head of my bed and sleep better than I have for years. I hold Labradorite while sitting in my chair every evening to remind me of proper posture and correct spinal alignment and I also carry a piece of Apache Gold in my pocket for overall good health. Currently I'm studying the physical realm of healing; tomorrow it's the exploration of the emotional and psychic realm of minerals.

Life should not only be a continual learning experience but an adventure. May there always be an Actinolite in your abundance corner and the proper mineral to guide you in your exciting journey through life.

~Larry L.

I celebrate that.
I appreciate your constant journey to wholeness, even when you cannot.
You are stronger after the breakage and the healing than you were in the first place.

Welcome home.

Ice

As a naturally occurring crystalline solid, I am considered a mineral, Hydrogen Oxide. I am the name given to any one of the 15 known crystalline solid phases of water. I am transparent or an opaque bluish-white color depending on the presence of impurities such as air or soil.

My most common transition is when water is cooled below 0 degrees Centigrade at standard atmospheric pressure. I can also be created from a vapor with no intervening liquid phase, such as frost. The word, Crystal, actually derives from a Greek word for frost.

I float on liquid water which is an important factor in Mother Earth's makeup. It has also been shown to be possible to superheat me beyond my melting point for short periods of time without melting me.

Until recently, it was commonly believed that Ice was slippery because the pressure of an object in contact with it caused a thin layer to melt, like the blade of an ice skate, exerting pressure on the Ice, melting a thin layer, and subsequently providing lubrication between the Ice and the blade.

This is not current theory and there is still much debate about why Ice is slippery. Now, scientists are believing that Ice molecules in contact with air cannot properly bond with the molecules of the mass of Ice and thus are free to move like molecules of liquid water. These molecules remain in a semiliquid state, providing lubrication regardless of pressure.

This phenomena described however, does not appear to hold true at all temperatures. Explorers in places such as Antarctica have reported that at very low temperatures snow loses its "glide", and pulling a sledge across it becomes like pulling a sledge through sand.

I am an unusual and mysterious being. I appear in nature as snowflakes, hail, icicles, glaciers, pack ice and the entire polar ice caps.

Emotional (Crystalline Grid) Bridge: I am regeneration. Pure and simple regeneration. I hold you in stasis so that you have time and a quieter breath to call out for all your resources when you most need them. Feeling me allows you to remember hope when it is utterly illogical.

Evolutionary Support: Water in all forms holds and cares for your emotions. When your memories are too painful, I will crystallize them until you are ready to look at them and accept them without judgment.

Tools for Co-Creation

When anger rises sharply within you
drink me.
Place me on the part of your body that swells with frustration.

I will help you to pause for a moment.
Breathe in my freshness.
This will give you a new perspective, maybe not possible otherwise.

Feel the cooling.
How does it affect your emotions?

Do you want to change anything?

Indigo Gabbro

I am from Madagascar. I am a particular medium to coarse-grained rock that consists primarily of Plagioclase Feldspar and Pyroxene. Essentially, I am the intrusive (plutonic) equivalent of Basalt, but where Basalt can be much the same, I can be varied. Iron and Titanium can be associated with me easily. Being from Madagascar, my oceanic form includes different and not yet specifically identified minerals that make up my Indigo coloring.

Emotional (Crystalline Grid) Bridge: Truth and unknown live together, though when you feel that now, you may want to hide from them. I see your bravery. You would not be here on the Earth, now, without it. Reach into it even if you don't believe that it exists or if you don't trust that you are as courageous as I already know you are.

How else will you know it?

Evolutionary Support: Wake up! You live in the vastness of the unknown while floating in the known...or at least the illusion of what could be known. I see you! I know you and I also let go of what I know so that I can be with you completely free to change each moment. In between your cells breathes infinite space—a whole universe—freely being, even as you define it with your measurements of millimeters and predictabilities. Nothing about you can be predicted. I welcome your universe!

Tools for Co-Creation

Hold me! I am here and now with you, because I choose that.
That is how you can even find me; it is your defined GPS to locate me.
And yet, I also exist far beyond all of this.
We live in many, many dimensions—some we haven't even explored yet!!!!
You have so many possibilities within you and therefore, before you, now.
Many of them seem hard and desperate, to you.
This simply offers you crystal clear motivation to change— to grow, to come fully alive!
It is your time. You can try to avoid it, yet it will not avoid you.
Join with your multi-dimensions.
You exist in endless worlds.
Simply soften the edges of this one world, regularly, and
that will lead you to your other selves in other universes, simultaneously.
All of you wants to know all of you.
Do it. Be it. You will of course simply find us there and
what a magnificent reunion that will be!!!

Jet

I am a form of fossilized wood, said to be of the Monkey Puzzle tree which flourished about 180 million years ago. I have been used throughout history as a highly prized and highly polished jewelry. In fact I can be so highly polished that I have been used as a mirror. I am lightweight, burn like coal and have traces of Aluminum, Silica and Sulphur and am classified as a mineraloid. I have been known historically in both hard and soft forms and much has been written of both. My hard form is said to be of carbon compression and salt water and my soft form of carbon compression and fresh water. I produce an electric charge when rubbed and have been known historically to possess medicinal qualities when ingested in water or wine.

Emotional (Crystalline Grid) Bridge: Softness comes in so many ways. I squeeze mine into your heart if you will stretch past your mind-alone to receive it. I look hard; I am full of blackness, yet my energy glides over and through you, with sinewy grace and ease. Feel past your beliefs and find me there.

Evolutionary Support: I smooth your edges. I soften your armor. Whatever you choose to do with this is up to you. I trust you.

Once you feel ease within, you relax. You breathe with extra space and elegance. Your breath brings you visions and your muscles flex to make them so. Everything within you pulses within the heartbeat of Life.

Once you feel ease within, you will attract more. If you do, I offer it.

Tools for Co-Creation

I am hard and I am soft.
I am hard where I need to hold together the edges of something precious.

I am soft where I greet the world and its endless gifts.
I am all things in perfect unmeasured measure.

To co-create with me, touch every part of you.
Enter the stillness.
You already live there.
Know yourself.
Ask to meet every part of you;
receive all that you are as graciously as you can.
Every part of you serves you. They serve you graciously.

I will co-create with you from the fullness of what you are.
And, as we do this, you will refine your being.
You will smooth your edges and soften your worries.
Life automatically gives you everything you need to graciously sculpt yourself.

Kangchenjunga Quartz

I am Quartz, specifically from the Nepal side of the Kangchenjunga Mountains. I come from an area where Aquamarine and many other minerals are also found. More importantly, I am clear and free and offer my services to the West (and everywhere else) for peace. It is not easy to get to where I live. Or back. I am a practice.

Emotional (Crystalline Grid) Bridge: Here I am, clear and free. It is the season of tremendous evolution and dangerously wondrous possibility for all of us. I am new with all that newness. I have evolved and am evolving. Put that into your heart. Embrace it with all of your being, now.

Evolutionary Support: I come from a part of the Earth Mother that has long held the inspiration and the support for the highest potential of the human species. I am part of that support and have been for as long as your species has been here.

If you hold me in your heart right now, you will feel the pureness of your evolution as it is coming, as it is you. That is what I offer you.

Tools for Co-Creation

I will ground you if you allow it.
Feel me entering your toes and pressing them smoothly and insistently into the Earth
as the roots they have always wanted to be.
I will release pain and struggle from all around you, if you allow it.
Feel me entering your heart and loving all your brave, evolving journeys.
Every part of you is well-deserving and utterly loved.
I am inspiring all of you, if you allow it.

Personal Story

My extraordinary Nepalese Quartz crystal arrived yesterday. Words cannot describe what a powerful experience this was. It feels like a sacred tool. It seemed to indicate that it wanted to be in the studio assisting me. I placed it on my studio altar set up to assist with my Periodic Table project. The quartz is taking the energy of all the other stones I have placed on this altar and it feels like a divining rod, directing all the powerful energy towards my working area.

This particular stone feels like a conduit between heaven and earth; with the larger horizontal crystal the earth plane, and the smaller crystal pointing to heaven. It's just perfect in terms of its representation of what the Periodic Table represents. The green color is so serene and I love the snow like effect on the surface of the crystal. The incised lines on the different planes of the crystal feel like encoded information. I have never worked or even held a laser crystal before. It is so powerful

(con't on next page)

Listen to me. Be ready. Act upon it.
Blessings, always blessings.

Personal Story

We have had so many journeys with Himalayan Quartz that were almost impossible. It drew us to our Brahman friend, whom we did business with for years before we had ever met. And from a business standpoint alone, it was crazy to buy this quartz. It's true, it was utterly exquisite, but it was a lot more expensive than other quartz that we could get. Besides that, when we first started buying these crystals, we had to pay by international wire transfers, which going to Nepal, then, were tricky to say the least. I remember our business banker saying that our wire had to go through three or four intermediaries before it could even arrive at our friend's bank. She stared me down, "Every time your money goes through even one intermediary, it is possible that it might stop there and just disappear forever."

The money we were sending was a lot, but we trusted. We trusted because the crystals had asked us to do it.

Tohmas and I wired the money to our new Nepalese friend right away; we wanted to get the stones as soon as possible because it was right before we would be vending at the biggest gem and mineral show in the world: The Tucson Gem Show. For us, it's our biggest expenditure and our biggest money-maker of the entire year by a huge percentage. We really wanted to have the quartz for that.

It took several days longer than expected for the wire to land, and the show had already started, but the wire transfer arrived safely. He immediately shipped us the quartz which we had bought (sight unseen!) from the Ganesh Himal Mine and the Kanchenjunga Mine, high in the Himalayas.

Towards the end of the show, we got the Nepalese quartz. We put it next to the poster of pictures of the young miners carefully, hand-harvesting the crystal treasures. They were exquisite! They were so unique and so incredible that we sold out of all of them within one and a half days: we have never had stones come and go so quickly, before or since.

That was our first experience with the Kanchenjunga Quartz.

Now we have many years of experience listening with and buying and selling this incredible quartz. It has touched our hearts so thoroughly that it

to the touch. I was holding it yesterday and the palm of my hand and heart chakra were vibrating so strongly.

The stone also seems to have been sent as a teacher. It feels like it has entered my life at the perfect time. Why am I even surprised?

Marilyn, thanks again for listening to your extraordinary stones and having the special gift of assisting this stone to find its way into my life. I feel so incredibly humbled and blessed.

With much love and gratitude to you and Tohmas.

~Rebecca K.

is a part of our being. It even brought us directly to Nepal, where we listened to them in person, under the guiding eyes of a tall, gold Buddha!

We heard the stories firsthand of how kindly these crystals are "birthed." They are hand-harvested only. Our friend's father was the one who started the mining of these crystals, not because he was a miner, but because he wanted to fund the opening of nine schools in his small part of the country (which he did!).

Our friend told us all the stories from his mining background. The miners would only gather the stones, after they directly asked the mountain for permission. If she said "Yes," they trekked up over 10,000' in altitude and took days harvesting stones with tiny hammers as their biggest tools. It takes infinite care and complete presence (and rituals and prayers from their holy people) to do this work and this utter respect is directly imbued in each of these gorgeous crystals.

Even after the quartz has been harvested, there is still so much more work. Each crystal is meticulously hand-wrapped and then placed in tightly woven baskets that are placed on the miners' backs for the long, tedious trip down.

Every time we see even one of these crystals arrive intact, we marvel: It has come through so much. It is a glittering miracle and we greet every one of them. They sparkle so magnificently, just knowing that they have been honored utterly at every step of their journey. Wouldn't you?

We have seen many Kanchenjunga Quartz clusters find homes with pleased people all over the world. They have heard the many stories of how beautifully the crystals have been treated and of the completely unique, Elemental, inspired gifts that they bring to everyone with whom they have contact (Even our business banker is impressed!).

Just for now, there seem to be no more clusters. We are a little sorry not to see them light up our lives right now, but all is fine. They have given us so much that it has spilled over into every part of our beings. How could we be anything but grateful . . . .

The Earth Mother is ever generous. We recently heard from our Nepalese miner friend who is very excited because there has been a new find at the Kanchenjunga Mine. Instead of the quartz clusters that were customary there, they have discovered quartz points—good sized and included with other minerals. He sent us one so that we could listen to its story:

Personal Story

Hawk's Eye Velvet Tourmaline.

I call this my time travel stone and I have had many remarkable journeys with this stone! I bought my first one during a workshop with Marilyn & Tohmas after hearing them tell the story of the geologist who found them and it has lived in my car ever since. I have asked this stone for help when I'm running late or traffic is particularly congested. Things always shift after I ask for help.

My favorite story with this stone is when I went to meet my friend Daniel for a cup of coffee. I was parked on the street right outside the coffee shop just getting ready to get out of the car when my cell phone rang. It was Daniel asking where I was. This wouldn't have been anything to comment on except Daniel was standing inside the coffee shop staring directly at me. He didn't see me even after I told him he was looking directly at my car. I took the stone inside with me and when I brought it out to show him I could see the

(con't on next page)

"It is the season to come out from the Earth, to bring the inner wisdom to the outer selves. Listen. I am part of you. I have just appeared because I am the sage within you that must come out now. Whether you can see it or not, humans have been brewing new wisdom through the ages. It just takes timeless patience, and then it always appears, just like me."

"Hold me. I am part of your new knowingness. In the core of your being, you feel that life on the Earth must be different— that all must change and the only change that touches everything is transforming your heart. This is the season for your heart to evolve beyond the measure of technology, or computing, or mechanical communication alone. I herald the new heart that is rising in your body and in your being. When you see me, feel your heart. This is the truth. The only way that you can prove it is to believe it. Then it will jump into your reality and it will change everything. The transformation is coming: May it come from the center of the Earth and from the center of our feelings— we will be well-guided."

Life and the Earth constantly surprise and honor us. Everything is changing. We choose to change with it and these are the miracles that we witness, and we share them with you, now and the miracles just keep growing.

~Marilyn and Tohmas T.

air around us get kind of wavy like all the particles of matter vibrating instead of appearing solid. At that moment I could see and feel how everything is constantly in motion.

~Allison A.

Kimberlite

I am named after the town of Kimberley in South Africa. I am known for containing diamonds. I occur in vertical "pipes" which are the main source of mined Diamonds today. These classic carrot-shaped pipes are called dykes or diatremes and can contain large amounts of carbon dioxide and/or water. It is assumed that I come from great depths within the Earth Mother and have been violently erupted towards the surface at some time. Only about 1 in 200 Kimberlite pipes contain any gem quality Diamonds. I am also a common carrier of Garnets and Chromium Diopside.

Emotional (Crystalline Grid) Bridge: Hard. Strength. Struggle. Power beneath all things, all moments. Who are you? Are you shaped by what goes on all around you?

Evolutionary Support: I hold pressure. I hold possibilities. I hold strength. I hold stress. I hold darkness. I hold constant growth. I hold the screams of the unknown.

Tools for Co-Creation

Are you ready to burst?
You are a being of utter transformation on a planet of utter transformation.
Everything you are is being stretched beyond yourself.
All your views are changing even if you don't like it.
Hold me.
Keep me in your pocket.
Grab me when you feel that if you grow anymore you will explode.
Explode with me!
Shout to the stars.
Scream into the Earth.
We will explode together.
It will be our spectacular birthing
and we will hold each other close—
so that we can still know love when we change beyond ourselves.

Kutnohorite

I am a rare mineral of Calcium, Manganese, Magnesium and Iron. I crystallize as massive to bundled blades of white through rose pink to light brown forms. My lovely pink shades are due to my increased manganese content. When I am browner, it is due to an increase of iron. I am a soft mineral and was named for the place I was found in 1901, Kutna Hora, Bohemia, Czech Republic. I have also been found in Italy and South Africa.

Emotional (Crystalline Grid) Bridge: I'm crying. I cry for all the pain that you make and that you live in. My heart weeps for you so that you will not be alone no matter what.

Evolutionary Support: I am a mystery. I am a mystery onto your mind and everything that you think about. When you feel what is hard in you, you will find me.............

Tools for Co-Creation

I am quite soft.
Can you feel that?

Even if you can't touch me with your hand,
reach out to me with your heart.
Find me
caress me
oh so gently
softly
in infinite care.

When your hardness and your uncertainties
meet
my fragility,
what happens?

What will you integrate
from our meeting?

What happens to your hardness . . . . .

Lemurian Seed Crystals

I am Quartz. I have been specifically found and named in Brazil and Russia. I tend to be recognized by the mostly horizontal growth lines that are particular to my family of being. I am on the cover of this book. Welcome.

Emotional (Crystalline Grid) Bridge: It is the season for me to stand powerfully before you. Please, listen to my heart. I show you that to grow strong and true we must grow with the Earth. We must honor her. It is how we best honor ourselves.

Evolutionary Support: Welcome. It is our wondrous time to truly come together. We have stories for you (and for us!). We offer you gifts and witnessing from beyond this Earthstar to root into this Earth Mother. Whenever you hear our stories and our unbounded love for you— for us—

please.

absorb them throughout your body. Let them caress every cell. Feel their flow from bone, to blood, to tooth, and more. Our gifts will breathe into each part of your body that has need and then willingness to be whole... to be free.

This is a season of healing for you— for us— and we join in that, as much as you allow. Open your hearts brightly-wide and we will find each other again and again and again,

Now,

ever now.

Personal Story

Last year a friend felt there was a really special stone waiting for her so she asked me to contact Marilyn and find out who was calling to her. What responded was a Lemurian Cluster that was abundant in every way but in the way of money, outside her budget.

This year she made a similar request. This time, Marilyn sent a list of several stones back to her. Number 2 on the list was the Cluster. There was no real draw for Maggie to this stone, but each time I came across the description, I felt drawn. Within two days of receiving that list, 3 very expensive stones left my life and moved on. One of the stones that left was a large single point Lemurian that I was pretty deeply attached to. It radiated one of the finest, most loving energies I have ever experienced and was stunned to find it ready to leave me.

I was pretty heart sick but realized I needed to respect this turn of events. When I wrote to Marilyn to ask what was responding for me since I had this sudden windfall of money,

(con't on next page)

Tools for Co-Creation

We are so honored to be here with you.
Your willingness allows this and it invites us to glide through your time and space
to be here. We are gloriously astounded by your presence; it offers endless possibilities, and within your world, you don't even "know" that— there is no concrete proof, that you understand, that exists within your agreed-upon paradigm.
We honor you. We respect you. We thank you with all of our beingness.
We recognize and accept that it is a blissfully rare and precious miracle that we meet here—at all—
in this way.
Please
before we co-create even more (again, we are profoundly honored!)
please
absorb that you are co-creating with us.
The simple truth that we are here, together, means that we have already co-created much and that we are continuing to co-create even more, and then ever more, as you wish and as you allow unconditionally.

Overflow your cells with this precious knowingness.
Drink of it passionately!
Fill your liver, your hair, your *smile* with it.
Feast on the wonder!

We will talk more. We are co-creating more.
Thanks and honoring to you, to us.

Personal Story

One summer Tohmas and I went to Brazil to go see the Stonebeings that were calling us. They wanted us to go to touch the land and feel them in there before we brought them home to share with other people. From just a business standpoint alone, it didn't make any sense, but we trusted the Stones that we needed to go and listen to them where they came from in the Earth and we did.

wouldn't you know it, it wasn't a single Lemurian point, but that sneaky Lemurian Cluster. Turns out, that all along the Cluster was patiently waiting for me to welcome it home and the money I received for my three stones was more than enough to cover the cost of a cluster I thought I could never afford.

~Cari W.

Once there our Brazilian friend kindly took us to the new Lemurian mine. What a wonder! The crystals were embedded in the clay and the miners were freeing them out with high-pressure water, alone. It was incredible to see and to feel the Lemurians being birthed so easily, simply and gracefully.

After we got to gently pull out one or two lasers, ourselves, we went and sat on a quiet hill away from the mine. We slipped naturally into a meditation that just enveloped us like a hug.

While I was savoring the view of the mountains and hills, I could feel the sky opening up to me. Past clouds and past colors, warmth melted into me. It was just so easy to relax ('Hope I remember this later!'). Almost before I could understand what was being said, I realized that I was listening to Pleiadeans who were just automatically talking with us:

This is the time and place for us to meet. We know each other so well, but it doesn't matter whether you remember or not. Do not strain to understand or recall. What matters is that we are here, together. Now.

As we speak with you, please absorb our energy and our gifts. We have been watching how humans are growing and learning and we know that we can help you to integrate everything that you are taking in so rapidly. Everything seems to be coming at you so quickly and so powerfully that you are shell-shocked in your immediate capacity to actually digest and use the marvels that you are receiving.

We cannot help you learn. However we can hold your hand, and if you let us we can hold your heart so that you will steady yourselves and choose to be whole in all that you do and in all that you truly are. This we celebrate! This we honor so deeply there are no words to offer; so we simply offer our energy, our love— knowing that you will then discover what we are feeling and saying for yourself, in your own way, and in your own sweet words.

So here is our gift to you, Marilyn (which you will share this with Tohmas): Root deep, deep into the Earth. Steady yourself. Let your heart beat strongly but gently— that's where its fullest strength lies. Now root again.

This time the roots find new directions that you have never found before. Let profound lightning come out of every inch of your feet in all ways, in all moments (This is why your feet must completely absorb the Earth with all of their measure.).

We gift the lightning to Tohmas, who touches it with a human heart (otherwise it might not be possible or kind here) and because of his ever immediate, open link to you, it goes through your body and down into the Earth. It speaks to the Grid. It helps with stabilizing all communication there and perhaps most of all, it allows those stories to be translatable to all humans, wherever they are in their journey.

Thank you.

Through you we feel our presence land upon the Grid and find a home (It hasn't found as easy a home on the Earth for some time.). It links us, and we sigh. Our growth and our passions are beautifully, inexorably intertwined. The dance is alive between us! We are more and more linked and we can support each other through open-heart miracles that none of us has ever been able to imagine before: new imagination is being realized in us now.

Now, a further gift~ . . . .

Put your arms out in front of you, about waist-high, and touch the palms together. They will pray into each other. They will feel themselves with the energy that they are meant to hold and then to use. Whenever you do this full posture (toes to the earth, palms matched), you will be able to touch things with an aliveness that your dreams could not before find. And whether you realize it or not, it means that you and Tohmas will infuse everything (as it wishes) with a soothing inspiration that will help others to absorb our steadying so that they can grow faster and freer than what has been possible before. You all are about to change the laws of actions and responses and we will witness with pure delight and grounded acceptance.

I opened my eyes. Did I get that right? It seemed so easy that it was dream-like....I rooted myself and then I put my hands together, palm-to-palm. The skies opened wide like a grin! Colors swirled around, especially blue, green and yellow. They danced in different shapes and then they jumped from the sky into my palms.

Energy circled, circled, circled. It grew onto itself and then grew beyond, simultaneously. I knew that it was Tohmas' energy calling down the lightning, just as it was always meant to be, and I was allowing it to land, in my hands and into the Earth, to be used, to be given, to be shared. It was strong, clear, and focused, but not overpowering. I knew that this was something that our spirits had always known would be and that Tohmas' and my willingness to just come to Brazil had just now allowed all of this energy to now be available. We had helped it come home.

Tohmas and I were sitting away from the other people who were working for the mine, because we wanted to focus on receiving this energetic gift, without talking or having to do anything else. So it surprised me when the foreman (who seemed pretty business-like and not overly "social") specifically came over and started talking to us. He had to really work at it, because like everyone else there he spoke only Portuguese and we knew a little but not much.

It took a long while and constant clarifying, but he told us that two weeks before we came to the mine he saw beautiful lights in the sky; they were like nothing he had ever seen there before. He watched the "fireworks" in amazement, because they swirled and beamed very brightly for a long while: yellow, blue and green. It was like a northern lights display, except that it happened in the southern hemisphere!

We were absolutely astounded. Then he quietly told us that the lights were right over the top of the mine— that they were pointing at it directly and they were filling the crystals with some special attention and love. He knew from that point on, that the crystals were very unique, that they had something new to offer, though he didn't know what it was.

He just stared at us, without another word. He walked away without ever saying anything else to us.

We knew. Our breaths joined and we knew exactly what he meant. The fireworks were happening in our bodies, too. From that moment on, we could no longer say we didn't know what we were doing in Brazil.

Fast forward to now and writing this book~

It has been such a full-out adventure listening to the Stonebeings and writing this book with them. In a way the other two volumes of "Stones Alive!" just slipped out. They birthed themselves so beautifully we don't even remember labor pains.

This time was different. I don't know why. Every story seemed to bleed me dry as the desert around us. There was no thinking, there was no understanding— no bells going off saying, "This is it!" I had to climb a mountain every day, to get what the Stones were offering, and every day I woke up to a new, bigger mountain.

Personal Story

Zagai Mountain Quartz

The first time I saw one of these beauties was magickal. Many are heavily included by Astrophyllite fibers and clouds that seem to affect the morphology of the quartz itself. This creates a new crystal form, a dynamic evolution of "just quartz." Together, the crystal and its inclusions create a very lively flow, energizing to the core. Whenever it decides to come out and play, my friends always seem to notice a change in my own energy. It feels like the brilliant sun and mountain air converge with some other, fiery quality.

I enjoy the mysterious component of these crystals. They are thought to contain traces of rare earth elements, and they have been one of my earliest introductions to these energies. It is something different altogether. They feel like they reach deep into us, and show us the starlight from which we are made. They seem to effect healing on a cosmic, cellular level. I have worked with my own Zagai

(con't on next page)

Yes.

I know there is an incredible, sacred opportunity being birthed here, the mountain speaks for that. But am I climbing too relentlessly to see the wide-open beauty of it?

Then the dawn came back to me.

In the first two books, the stones spontaneously appeared. They poured their open hearts to us. We listened. We recorded their precious stories and then we shared them with as many people around the world as possible. It was, and is, sheer delight.

Now that the Stonebeings had offered that, it was time for us to join with them even more. The stories were being birthed in their bodies and our bodies, simultaneously. The Stonebeings gave us everything they had. They were used to this, (We were used to it, too!) and they did it beautifully. And then they waited— they paused.

They were waiting for our part. This book is a co-creation. It is a union of stone and human. It is no longer just about what they can offer us, alone. We were holding their stories in our hearts and all that was needed was to add our stories, our energy, our wide-open hearts reaching into the vast unknown.

Of course it felt different. Of course we had to climb the mountains.

For me (Marilyn) I had to root myself more than I have ever done before. Tohmas was calling in the lightning, as he does so beautifully, so constantly. Then I had to clasp my hands together. The Stonebeings blessed them— they blessed them so that the words flowing from our fingertips would land here as an unconditional marriage of our species. That is the evolution awaiting each human now. Can we truly give our hearts to embracing all the other forms of life upon the Earth Mother? Isn't that why we are here? This glorious book speaks our most destiny, out loud, for all to hear.

The cover of "Stones Alive! 3" reminds us of the lights in the Brazilian sky blessing the Lemurian Seed Crystals there, as the new mine foreman described. This gorgeous picture is telling us every day that the Stonebeings have been imbued with a special energy that comes to us humans now, to help us evolve, when we so desperately need it.

It is our story too, our personal story. Listening to the Stones for this incredible book is our evolution. We have had to listen as never before and

Quartz for clearing mental blocks and seeing the things we often choose not to see. It feels like a swirling cloud that helps us journey astrally and grow emotionally, all the while supporting our physical systems. These crystals are very unique, and I expect that they will be a part of the awareness of the Earth Mother's evolution.

~Nick P.

we have had to co-create with the Stones and the Earth Mother with more of our hearts than ever. We don't necessarily know how to do it, but we are doing it. These pages live as proof and walk in the world as glorious affirmation.

We offer this book and our story from the core of our heart. It's not easy to talk about it, but we are. Just like the Stonebeings, we are pouring out our essence here and you will decide to accept this precious gift or not. But if our experience means anything, it is giving us the immediate opportunity to evolve, to listen to the Stonebeings for ourselves (not just to read about it somewhere) and to put everything into it.

That is the invitation, the initiation and the new, gorgeous, vast mountain before us.

~Marilyn and Tohmas T.

Lepidochrosite

I am Iron Oxide Hydroxide. I am usually red to reddish brown and tend to form when iron rusts underwater. I am found in the weathering of primary iron materials and in iron ore deposits. I can be commonly found as rust scale inside old steel water pipes and water tanks. I was first described from a deposit found in the Czech Republic in 1813. I can be found in many many places and am similar to Goethite, Hematite and Limonite.

Emotional (Crystalline Grid) Bridge: Let's flash together! Let's jump, eyes-open, into the fracas of whatever adventure Spirit is showing us right now . . . . .

Evolutionary Support: I twirl. I sparkle. I wink. I am just like the child in you (go ahead and deny it, but it's still true, true, true!). I am free to give and receive love in any imagination that will hold it for a breath or a smile.

Tools for Co-Creation

If you are a child and someone is reading this to you,
tickle them.
Tell them that the Lepidochrosite in you made you do it!
(And if you can say THAT, you're magicalmysticalsplendid!)

If you are an adult and you are reading this,
I am talking to you:

You will never really grow up.
You might make your hair sparkle silver.
You might tell me "SPEAK UP! I can't hear you!"
You might even stop somersaulting down bumpy hills
on purpose.

But
your heart will stay young.
It is a child.
It is always a child.
It talks fast when it's excited.
It runs with kids any age, just as long as there is someone to play with
you.

Your heart is your child and the child-you is your heart.

I know you know that.
Your heart never forgets.

Libyan Desert Glass

I am a controversial substance found in areas of the Libyan Desert as well as in deserts in other parts of Africa and South Australia. I am also called Edeowie glass or great sand sea glass. Chemical analysis proved that I am not a Tektite but made of the same sand as the desert. But no one really knows how I was melted and I contain no water because of the extremely high temperatures involved. It is said that the Australian glass was created by an atomic bomb. It is postulated that ancient civilizations created this glass and what we find now are the remains of those human technological societies. We even have a current process called Brown's Gas that has been ignored by science that could easily have been available in those times to create the high temperatures needed to produce this glass. It is also currently postulated that I have been created by huge fireball explosions in space. You will need to decide for yourself. I am usually of a yellow to yellowish green color and I was also found by Vincenzo de Michele in the middle of one of Tutankhamen's necklaces and dated to well before his time.

Emotional (Crystalline Grid) Bridge: Life lies out before us. Its reach is endless and its inspiration vast. You are so taken by your own gasps of fear and admiration, that you don't notice me. You probably don't see the other beings that walk beside you in every step.

I am with you. I will always be with you, in some way, in some form. Neither of us knows how that will happen or what it will look like.

Evolutionary Support: This is a season of great change. I grow that change in my cells. Feel me. Meditate upon me (even if you can't find a piece of me to hold, as well). Across time and space upon the Earth Mother, we all can travel them more than you ever realized before.

Find me!

See what I am. We are beings of great change. How will we keep finding each other?

Tools for Co-Creation

I know that you have decided a great many things in your life.
And many of your decisions are habits—
That way when life hands you something difficult, you have an array of stock answers that you can give without feeling anything (especially fear).

Personal Story

Many years ago during an astrological reading I was given the following information: "Everything tells you its story: animals, trees, stones. And your mission on earth is to tell their stories through your art". I wasn't quite sure what this meant until years later, when I had the following experience.

I received a phone call from a woman identifying herself as a steward of a collection of meteorites that belong to a shaman in New Mexico. The Shaman had passed away and left instructions for the meteorites to be distributed to healers throughout the world, who could take the encoded information in the stone and use it to assist others. I told the woman she must have the wrong person, that I was an artist not a healer. She informed me that I had the gift to heal people through my artwork. As we continued talking she was dowsing the paired meteorites. One of the sets responded very strongly as we spoke, and she offered to send them to me.

(con't on next page)

You just answer so that nothing really startles you.

You and your ready-made answers live safely.

But will you grow?
Will you stretch tall into the big, bad, beautiful newness that visits you
each moment?
Will you be what's next for you, even though you don't already know it?
Let me ask you a few questions.
Carry them with you, if you like.
Read them to yourself before sleeping without thinking about them—
just burn them into your dreamtime awareness for effect.
Ask them to answer themselves when they are ready.
There is no time limit and there are no wrong answers.

Ready?

Go:

1. Who are you today?
2. What do you want to be more than anything else?
3. How will you be whatever you most want to be?
4. When will you be whatever you most want to be?
5. What are your favorite things about you?
6. If you could be called by any name, what would it be?
7. Can you look in the mirror twice a day and say "Yes!!"?
8. What understanding of the world do you have right now that you can just let go of and then feel the freer for its release?
9. What were you like the moment you were born?
10. At the end of the day: What are the most incredible things you have felt today?
11. What gifts have you given yourself?

Several days later two meteorites arrived in a burgundy cloth pouch. I called to thank the woman and asked her how to work with the stones. I was told if I listened to them they would guide me. I held one in each hand and sat quietly on a bench in my garden, falling into a deep meditative state. I am not even sure how long I was sitting holding the meteorites, when my eyes opened. A strong feeling came over me to go to my studio and draw. I started doing what would be described as automatic drawing. It was as if I was being directed by the stones to give them a visual voice on paper. I had never worked this way before. It was astounding to me the speed of the evolution of the forms on the paper. One of the drawings was sent to the woman as a thank you. After viewing the drawing I was told, "The Universe knew you would know what to do with these meteorites." Additional meteorites were also sent, and they have inspired a series of drawings entitled: Meteoritic Messages.

This experience was pivotal in the development of my stone

(con't on next page)

awakening. Over the years I have been blessed with the gift of travel to ancient places collecting rocks that speak to me. The creation of art continues to provide a wonderful vehicle to share the stones' messages with others.

~Rebecca K.

M

Mesolite

I am a member of the Zeolite family of minerals and I closely resemble Natrolite. I occur in void fillings in Basalt. I have a hardness of 5 to 5.5 and my first described occurrence was in the Cyclopean Islands by Sicily. My name comes from the Greek word for middle. I am usually white to pale grey or yellow and can commonly occur as needles or threads or hairs.

Emotional (Crystalline Grid) Bridge: Do you feel it? So many things will come to you in your life. They all are gifts. Will you let your Spirit show you that? Will you let yourself believe it? I know that many of the gifts will land like devastation to your pride. Will you feel gashed? Will you also know the sweet honing beneath each scar?

Evolutionary Support: There is nothing that must be done. Let's simply be together. Peace. Breathe. Stillness. I offer these. When I do, it's a clear call for your mind to unwind, to let go of the chatter that has taken over itself.

Tools for Co-Creation

I am that I am.
I am that I am.
I am that I am.

Monazite

I am a reddish brown mineral containing many rare earth metals including important sources of Thorium, Lanthanum and Cerium. There are actually four different kinds of me depending on my elemental composition. I can also contain small amounts of Uranium as well as a significant amount of Helium, which can be extracted by heating. I can be radioactive and am found in large placer deposits in India, Madagascar and South Africa. My name means "to be solitary."

Emotional (Crystalline Grid) Bridge: All is one. We are one. Perhaps more importantly to your kind journey, you are one. All of you is one.

Evolutionary Support: Chant with me. When we chant, everything will still. Then everything will dance with its unique shimmy. The Crystalline Grid will sing. It will record our every Ohm and every echo. A chorus of everything-anything will land in the Grid and miracles will be born of unexpectedness.

Tools for Co-Creation

I know that every day you have many things to do.
Soon your list of To Do's will grow more and keep growing.
It is the distraction that your species offers to its fear.

Breathe.
You can do what I suggest here or not.
You will not be greater or lesser for it; you will be different— because you are different in each moment regardless.

Try not doing anything.
Just be.
If you can't focus on that, chant my name.
I will chant with you, too.
Don't worry if you don't hear me.
Just keep chanting.
Something will happen.
Something unexpected will open your heart.

N

Nuummite

I am Anthophyllite, a Magnesium rich Amphibole, a variety of Asbestos. I am specifically from Greenland but have been found in many states in the U.S. also. I am usually greenish to brown and can have spreads of slender fibrous golden streaks.

Emotional (Crystalline Grid) Bridge: You think you know some things, but you don't know how to do them, in wisdom. Those are your defenses talking, because if you absorbed how endlessly knowing you are, you would EXPLODE with enlightenment.

Evolutionary Support: Endless breezes of time pass through me. I have seen all the ages; I have tasted their sweetening sorrows. To me, they all are food that gives me precious, perfect lifeforce. I turn away from none of it. I enter the fullness of every Earth experience. They shape my being so that I grow strong, even when they crack me open and I must start all over again in my forming.

Whatever comes to me teaches me who I will be now; yet I leave behind nothing. All the gifts that I have ever received are the cells of my body. They tell the stories of every feeling, every sigh, every twinkle, every mystery. I am not given what I need to survive, for I don't need to survive. Yet, graciously, I am given everything I need to thrive, to turn my soul to the Sun in echoing goldness,

and I blossom.

Tools for Co-Creation

Take me with you
everywhere.
I am not fragile.
I witness EVERYTHING with quiet and bright eyes.

To truly see and feel all that happens here imprints my soul
with endless stories.
Each story, no matter how infinitesimal, brings vast wisdom that nurtures lifeforce
even when it seems otherwise.

Everything here cares for me.

If you care for me, I will show you how everything else does the same for you
even when it seems otherwise.

Onyx

I am a cryptocrystalline form of Quartz. My colors range from white to most every color and I can contain bands of certain colors. I am called Sardonyx when the bands are colors of red instead of black. My pure black form is common and famous and my hardness is 7. I can be confused with much softer banded materials commonly used to try to imitate me because they can be more readily available. Agate is also sometimes stained in an attempt to to imitate me. My name originally is an Assyrian word meaning, ring.

Emotional (Crystalline Grid) Bridge: Purity. You are surrounded by pure, unconditional life in everything in each moment. There are no adequate words for this, so I just bring you this energy, now.

Evolutionary Support: I come to you and I fill your aura with peaceful clarity whenever you invite me. I am the loving pause before you act. I am the consideration before you do what you are thinking. Sometimes I am an almost instantaneous breath that reminds you to always, always remember the Spirit-that-moves-in-all-things. Sometimes I am a meditation, a vision quest, where you will travel all worlds to learn what you must know now— who you must be now.

Feel it......I am the breeze that brings the air that you breathe in. When you breathe with infinite caring, then that air turns to prana in your body and your being. I watch this and I affirm its splendor with all my heart.

Tools for Co-Creation

Keep me nearby.
Touch me as often as you can
When you do, you remember, tangibly,

that Body and Spirit dance as one.
They both bring forth unique graces that balance
in,
with,
around
all things.

When I am with you,
your bones settle into the knowingness of this.
You form your body
around it and
with it:

A conscious body brings consciousness to all of life!

Pearl

I am produced within the inside soft tissue of a living, shelled mollusk. I am Calcium Carbonate in crystalline form. I can form in fresh water as well as salt water. I can form without human intervention or I can be "grown" (cultured) on a pearl farm. I am created, in a sense, in the same way as the inner part of the shell (Mother of Pearl or Nacre) is created. I am rare in my true iridescent form and have been searched for constantly.

Emotional (Crystalline Grid) Bridge: I am always here, accepting you completely. When you think that you are beyond any redemption or any possibility at all, call me. That is what I was created for and from. I come as an unconditional gift to the children of the Earth, especially the human children. I know you stew in your own hurtful, emotional juices. Call on me and I will offer you my heart.

Evolutionary Support: I seamlessly, sweetly merge with you. I care for you. I see the struggles and I trust that they will twist and turn and change. Everything cycles endlessly, gorgeously. If you like, I will smile and hold your hand and your heart while we breathfully watch the turn of events and feel all of the emotions that come along with the tide.

Tools for Co-Creation

I have no need to do something.
I am.

Together we will simply be.

We are here because we have consciousness.
If something else wishes to flower from that,
we utterly allow it.
With our complete allowability life flowers—
we its endless petals.

Personal Story

Pollucite

One time at the Tucson Gem Show, Tohmas came up to me and placed a stone in my palm and clasped my hand over it so that I couldn't see it. Immediately, I felt my entire body accelerate, as if I were on a glorious ride that would take me right up to heaven.

Instinctively I put the stone on my third eye: It was home. It loved it there! It cleared my vision and suddenly I could breathe so well that everything around me also clarified and brightened. I was enamored with looking at everything and anything in their new, vivid hues.

I gave him the Stone back and heard myself, saying, "It is a Stone for breatharians. It turns breath into prana." He immediately bought a lot of it so that we could share it with as many people as possible, which we did. We loved watching them putting it on their third eye and traveling anywhere they wished!

Several weeks later, Tohmas decided to google this new

(con't on next page)

Be
Be
Be

Pollucite

I am a Zeolite mineral with Iron, Calcium, Rubidium and Potassium as substituting elements. I generally form in colorless, white, grey or sometimes pink or blue masses. I have a hardness of 6.5 with brittle fracture and no cleavage. I typically occur in Lithium rich Granite pegmatites. I was first described in 1846 when found on Elba Island in Italy and am named for the mythological Pollux, twin brother of Castor, because I am often found with Petalite (which was previously known as Castorite.). I have been found in Europe, Russia, Namibia, Canada, and the USA.

Emotional (Crystalline Grid) Bridge: You are your breath crystallized into form, into action. Inhale completely and your heart swings open. Exhale freely and your heart urges your body to let go of the old pain that haunts it.

Evolutionary Support: I am a Stone of breath. When you invite me in, I inhale with you. I exhale with you. According to your free intent, I stretch their possibilities. I fill your body with greater breath. I light up the shadows within, with pure prana, of your own making. Prana is your lifeforce merging with all life and accepting more.

Tools for Co-Creation

Hold me.
Watch your breath. Let it travel freely. Just see where it goes.
Where does it start?
Where's the last place it touches before it leaves you
What's its rhythm like? (Don't change it.)Is it even? Does it whistle?

stone that we didn't really know anything about. He grinned when he printed out the read-out for me. The most active ingredient in this stone that supported breathing was oxygen!

~Marilyn and Tohmas T.

What happens to the different parts of your body when breath fills them?
Do your bones ache?
Do your bruises settle?
How do you digest your food then?

With me as your friend, we can watch your breath.
You have controlled it too long.
It wants to be a free traveler in your life; it has so many gifts to give —you don't even know what they will all be.

Watch.
Listen.
Breathe.

Watch.
Listen.
Breathe

Do not change your breath, until you have become great friends and you can ask it what to do next..........

Purpurite

I am pink to purplish red and can often have a brown or black tarnish. My hardness is only 4 to 4.5 as a Manganese Phosphate. I am somewhat rare and I tend to form with Heterosite. I then am the Manganese rich part and Heterosite is the Iron rich part. I also can contain parts of the original Lithiophyllite that I pseudomorphed from.

Emotional (Crystalline Grid) Bridge: Place me in your heart. Don't think about it. Place me in your heart any way that you can. When you feel me softly pulsating there, relax. Ease your nerves and put all of your sweetness into your breath.

I am creativity birthing in your heart.

I am your creativity growing in your heart.

I am all creativity blossoming through your body.

Evolutionary Support: How does a seed grow? Bit by bit, it stretches, and stretches just a little more. At first it seems that nothing is happening. Then in a single moment, a soft but strong sprout bursts out and twists through stones and dirt, reaching for a sun that it has never seen but has always felt within its soul.

I am a seed. The energy within me shoots out and touches the world. If it lands upon you then you remember: I am small but mighty. Everything that is needed to make miracles already breathes in me if I just stretch and stretch for the Sun!

Tools for Co-Creation

When I am nearby (or when you reach out across the Ethers and just say my name)
stop everything.
Root yourself fully into the Earth Mother.
Then twist, turn, and mightily stretch.
Feel your body spiral
soften
strengthen.

You are alive!
You are the stuff of miracles and kingdoms and pure magic
completely.

Call up that creativity in you.
Let it twist
turn
stretch
every day.

Let it take you to unknown roads
where you will find the adventure that even now
calls your name.

Sard

Much used by the ancients as a gemstone, I am a reddish brown Chalcedony. Pliny the Elder says that I am from Sardis, in Lydia, where I was supposedly first discovered. Others believe I was named this because they say I came from Persia which means sered, or yellowish red. I was used by the Assyrians for cylinder seals, by the Egyptians and Phoenicians as scarabs and by the early Greeks as gems. In Hebrew, the odem (which translates as sardius), which is the first stone in the High Priest's breastplate, was red and was believed to be Sard but could have been Carnelian or red Jasper. Some forms of me closely resemble Carnelian but I am usually much harder. My range of colors is great, going from orange to red to golden and I can even get so dark as to appear black. The ancients most valued my hyacinthine color.

Emotional (Crystalline Grid) Bridge: Life is filling you. You let go of it in every exhale so that you can drink in one thousand times more in every rich inhale. Allow. Completely allow. When you breathe out, hang onto nothing. When you breathe in, accept everything. That is the way of the heart.

Evolutionary Support: Today is the day to grasp your own vitality. Reach out every cell of you for it; stretch and soar all that you are until you land upon it (or until it lands upon you!). Savor it. Prize it. Feast upon it without pause.

I will reach out all my being to you and you will reach all your being to your unfiltered lifeforce. That's where we meet. That's where we grow.

Tools for Co-Creation

I know that I am a complete and honorable being.
When you are around me

or when you meditate upon me
or when you call out to me,
I am a complete and honorable being.
I will answer you; I will always answer you.
From the core of my respect I will bring you any support
that you will receive
that is also honoring your greatest vitality.
You will feel that
even if your old defenses shout above my words
or twist their meaning to justify turning them away.
I am still here.
I am a complete and honorable being.
I am here for you.

Scolecite

I am a hydrated Calcium Silicate of the Zeolite group. My name comes from the Greek work, skolec, which means "worm." I am a Calcium Zeolite unlike the Sodium Zeolite, Natrolite and the Sodium/Calcium Zeolite, Mesolite. I occur in fibrous aggregations where there is a plane but no axis of symmetry. I am usually colorless or white and am transparent. I have been found in Iceland, California, Scotland, Brazil and commonly in India.

Emotional (Crystalline Grid) Bridge: Give your full attention to yourself. While you receive all of life's generous initiations and regenerating retreats, offer yourself all the love you can possibly give.... and then, more.

Evolutionary Support: I am a being of healing. That does not mean I will take away your pain or that I will remove your imbalances. I smell them. I caress them. Sometimes I sit with them and just listen to their stories.

Healing happens whenever something unloved is listened to completely

right now.

Tools for Co-Creation

I have nothing to say.
I almost never have anything to say
because I find no great use in my words.
Instead
come and sit with me.
Do whatever you wish.
I don't need anything from you and I'm not asking you for anything that you don't want to give.
If you just want to come here and tell me your story,
then yes, I will listen.
You can insert the words here
whenever you like,
as much as you like
or as little as you like.
I will listen to the still-birthing-silences and grimaces, too.
You can change your stories every time you come here.
Or you can scream about the same pain
over and over again, to the point that no one else could possibly hear you.
I will listen. I will keep listening.
One now, you will say enough that you can empty yourself
into the fullness of complete listening
and that will heal you, if you wish, in any way you wish.

Sillimanite

I am one of three Alumino-Silicate polymorphs, Andulusite and Kyanite being the other two. One of my common varieties is known as Fibrolite because in that form I appear like a bunch of fibres twisted together and this can even be seen by the naked eye at times. I am an index mineral indicating a high degree of metamorphism and am used to determine the temperature, depth and pressure with which that occurs. I am also called Bucholzite at times and I was named after the American chemist, Benjamin Silliman. I am colorless to pale brown,

Personal Story

While gathering Graphic Stones in the mountains of central Arizona, I would watch the mule deer families watch me as I gathered select stones. An unusual pegmatite swarm produces this Graphic Stone and its pattern resembles hieroglyphic writing of some long forgotten script- messages traveling from the past for our use in the future.

One day, the mule deer were much more interested in something else, rather than me, under a large lone alligator juniper tree. I climbed a low ridge to get a better look at what was holding the deer's interest. The distinctive outline of the top of a mountain lion's head, ears up with a batman-like silhouette was faintly visible. As I crouched down and watched the motionless cat well camouflaged in the deep shade I noticed a cats-eye chatoyant gemstone scattered on the ground with a white to lime green color.

I gathered a few of the stones for identification and returned later to the spot to try and locate the source of the gemstone.

(con't on next page)

yellow or greenish. I am harder than Quartz and my first discovery was in the Czech Republic. I am also the official mineral of the state of Delaware.

Emotional (Crystalline Grid) Bridge: Innocence. Savor it. It is your original home.

Evolutionary Support: Can you find me? I am the white spaces between the words, the emptiness extending your exhales. I fill bottomless need.

I am a being of silence and invisibility. Perhaps it will never be possible to "show" you those things. When your struggle overcomes you, I will be there, like the remnants of a dream: fleeting yet constant, familiar yet ever unknown.

Tools for Co-Creation

To work with me, your need must spontaneously call me out.
I don't know how that will happen because you will shape it.
If I knew, it would mean that I was not truly open, not empty enough to fill freely.
You might not know how to find me or how to work with me because you don't know who or what you will be when the stress of living separation snaps you—
shatters your will.
Maybe you will not even be able to call out.
I come when you do not know why you are.
I come when fear overshadows your divinity and there is nothing left to love.
I come when you have shrunk into pain so completely that you cannot ask for anything
because you can no longer speak or think of help.
I will come when your struggle has wrestled so long
there is nothing left.
I am in the nothingness.

The gemstone was a rare cats-eye Sillimanite, an extremely hard gemstone, harder than quartz and related to ruby and sapphire. Cats-eye stones are protector or guardian stones. Since ancient times they have been used as protection during travel and also during the dream state.

I dug a small hole in following where I had originally found the Sillimanite while observing the mountain lion. Upon return to the site a few weeks later, the unmistakable odor of mountain lion marking its territory surrounded my activity. Realizing I needed to respect the overseer of this area a bit more, I made my visits to the area brief, alert, and the disturbance to the environment minimal and respectful.

~Robert P.

Stannite

I am a sulfide of Copper, Iron and Tin. I am an ore of Tin and am found mostly in hydrothermal vein deposits. I am also known as Bell Metal Ore. My color is blue to various shades of grey. My name is derived from the Latin word for Tin, stannum. I can occur in well formed crystals and have been found in Germany, Czechoslovakia, England, Russia, South Dakota, Bolivia, and Tasmania. I am similar to Chalcopyrite and Arsenopyrite.

Emotional (Crystalline Grid) Bridge: Yes, I understand. I realize that you do not always want to give the time and energy to truly feel everything around you. I know that your scars associate that with pain, even when some of your curiosity does not.

I understand. Whenever you are ready, you will reach out boldly and touch everything you can with your heart, and what a glorious reunion that will be!

Evolutionary Support: I usually connect with Animals, Plants and Stones. My heart does not immediately speak human, yet I am here at your request. To hear me now, listen in ways that you have not met before. Listen. And then listen, elsewhere.

Can you hear a whale crash through the water within my words? Do you smell the lavender growing strong in a field that you have never visited? Listen. Listen anew. Listen afield.

Tools for Co-Creation

I feel your loneliness.
I know that humans have evolved a little differently than anything else upon the Earth Mother. Still, it is also in your cells to hear everything:
everything.
Yet you feel differently enough that not everything lands upon you in the same ways that it does for every other Animal, Plant and Stone.
You are unique.

Personal Story

I had just finished a painful divorce that had taken 3 years. I was re-adjusting my life's journey. Feeling a desire of expanding my heart, I acquired a Rose Quartz (from the authors of this book). It was relayed from the Rose Quartz, in transit, thru Marilyn, that the heart expansion was occurring & there may be others. I had a brief relationship that encouraged me to take in a rescue dog, a white German Shepherd that came with the name of "Angel". The woman that had encouraged this, her last name was Shepherd. I am animal lover, however I had never met an animal that I was so connected with! A short period later I met a woman that I have had the fortune of having this same experience of the heart with.

All within a 2 year period, these Ladies, including the Rose Quartz, have my heart. This Rose Quartz has the soothing feeling of a rose petal caressing my heart. I have observed others in its presence with this incredible heart movement as well.

~Michael B.

This offers itself to you, and to all of life,
as a gift and a frustration.
They are the same, and for you, inexplicably different, too.
If you cannot find your sameness with every other child upon the Earth,
then listen to your differences.
What have they been saying so long that they drown out what you have in common with anything and everything?
I will wait here and record everything you explore, everything you are.

Stichtite

I am hydrated Magnesium Chromium Carbonate Hydroxide. My color is usually pink through to lavender purple. I am somewhat rare and was discovered in Tasmania and am named after the nearby mine owner. I am an alteration of Serpentine.

Emotional (Crystalline Grid) Bridge: I ground an easy space for feeling everything. If you cannot do what you must, ask for my energy. Keep insisting that my gifts join you. They will be there. They will be you.

Evolutionary Support: Let us enter our hearts together. Revel in the vastness and in the complete wisdom. Whenever you crave safety, come here. Just come here. You don't need to do anything. Just be here. Just be...with your heart.

We are home.

Tools for Co-Creation

I am so pleased to be here listening with you
speaking with you!
It soars my Spiritpossibilities until
I meet you in the sky of our dreams.

To co-create together,
we must land our dreams upon the Earth.
Then we carry them (safely adored in our hearts)
with us,
everywhere.
We must carry them quietly in all things that we do, think and say.

By carrying them with us
our bodies will answer our perseverance and they will tell us
how to make our dreams so
here and now
in every reality that we deserve.
They will tell us how to land them upon the Earth and upon our lives
step by step
breath by breath
impossibility into reality.

Listen with all your body.
It is speaking to me, to you, to us, now~

Personal Story

Our business has vended at the Tucson Gem Show for many years. Most business trade shows last three days: Friday, Saturday and Sunday. Not the Tucson Show, it's an all-out marathon. We prep for the Show, every single day, for weeks in advance and the show, itself, goes day and night for about twenty-one days straight. We absolutely love it and I would never trade away a second of it, but by the end, you feel like a runner who has been going uphill with a dozen packs on your back.

Our good friend, John, has been working with us during the Show for the last several years now. I agree with him when he says that there's always a lesson to be learned from Tucson, and he's not talking about business or selling things, he's talking about life. When you have to be that focused for that long, you WILL learn about something amazing about the bigger picture.

This year at Tucson I learned. And learned. And learned. I have never gotten so many opportunities, one after the other, to starkly review my life.

I love it. Looking at life at the core is my middle name. I even love it when it hurts my feelings, but I will admit that I got seriously sideswiped during this show. Remembering to breathe became a conscious activity, not a habit.

One day felt pretty rough. A couple of events socked me right in the ego. At the end of the day I was probably feeling pretty sorry for myself because I felt so alone. I was completely surrounded by people (and almost all of them unbelievably kind) and I couldn't see them. I was on my island and I was starting to wonder if I had anything useful to offer anyone.

During this, Tohmas was doing his part of the business—buying stones for us to sell to others. Tohmas is amazing. Things that I take personally just slide by him without a sideways glance. He knew I was surfing some wild waves, so he didn't say anything; he's respectful and gives me space so that I can learn what I need to without interference or attachment from anyone else.

I love that about him. Utterly and completely.

At the same time, the wounded little-girl-me might have been very happy if he would have stopped everything and tried to get me to smile. When I'm feeling sorry for myself, there are a whole lot of interesting scenarios running through my head that I don't actually want to have happen (I ain't THAT crazy), but sometimes I replay them just for the entertainment.

After my wild-ride day, we went back to where we were staying. I was a deflated balloon. He quietly gave me a heart shaped out of Serpentine. "Thanks." It was nice. Then he turned it over so that I could get a better look at it, and he said, "This one is especially for you." There inside the Serpentine heart was a tiny, natural, purple (my favorite color) Stichtite heart completely contained within the bigger, man-made heart. A miracle, it was a quiet, natural miracle right before my eyes.

I didn't have to be a Stone listener to know what it was saying. While I was "playing" at being alone, Tohmas found a heart-within-a-heart stone for me. When I felt that Stichtite, I knew the truth: I knew I was loved. I knew that I was not alone. I was a little heart inside of a much bigger, freer heart that was very quietly just holding me, just waiting for me to find the miracle that was already waiting for me.

I had that Stichtite heart with me the rest of the Show. I think that it will be with me forever.

~Marilyn T.

Stromatolite

I am layered accretionary structure formed by the binding and trapping of microorganisms, especially cyanobacteria, commonly known as blue-green algae. Ancient Stromatolites are common in the fossil record but are rare today. We were much more abundant in Precambrian times and many different fossil forms of me are available. The earliest confirmed origin of one of my forms is 2,724 million years ago. I can be found today in rare marine environments and when found they are called, "living fossils." Cyanobacteria are currently believed to be largely responsible for the increasing amount of oxygen in the early Earth's atmosphere through their photosynthesis thus participating in our evolution in an intimate fashion. Cyanobacteria use water, carbon dioxide and sunlight to create their food and the byproducts of this process are oxygen and lime. This banding of layers of limestone over time gives me my commonly recognized banded patterning. I am found in modern times in hyper-saline lakes and marine lagoons where high saline levels create extreme conditions that exclude animal grazing. Two of these locations are in Western Australia and Rio de Janeiro, Brazil. Fresh water Stromatolites can also be found in Cuatro Cienegas, and in very unusual places in the Mexican desert. My fossilized forms are common, as mentioned, in Australia and in Glacier National Park,U.S.A., among other places.

Emotional (Crystalline Grid) Bridge: When you are bone weary, feel this: Life cycles in and it cycles out. Whatever you need will come in the next wave and you are renewed.

Evolutionary Support: Eternal wisdom lives in me. Its sea floods over all doubts. Do you remember? Do you want to remember?

If you ask for it, it will fill your veins. It will crowd out your fears. That's how you will know I am with you even before you know I am with you.

Tools for Co-Creation

Place me next to your food. I will bless it, as you wish.
Place me next to your water. I will fill it with whatever joy that you ask me to give.

Place me next to your doorway. I will welcome everything unconditionally and support you in doing the same.
Place me in your garden. I will remember the sacredness in the soil and in anything growing and I will celebrate them!
Place me in your vehicle. I will honor movement and I will breathe with you so that you will transport yourself and others with presence and peace.
Place me next to the books you are reading. I will smile at the perfect knowledge there and I will add knowingness. Hold me as you read and I will bring you wisdom

if you wish.

Super Seven Crystals (also called Melody's Stone)

I am a combination of Amethyst, Clear Quartz, Smokey Quartz, Cacoxenite, Rutile, Goethite and Lepidochrosite. I am from Espirito Santo, Brazil.

Emotional (Crystalline Grid) Bridge: I am made up of so many things. That brings us such aliveness and we bring that to everything and everyone else.

Evolutionary Support: Welcome. I overflow with gratitude to work with you, now— for that is why we are here. I come to you to work with you, to consciously co-create the world that your Spirits breathe into your dreams.

Tools for Co-Creation

Welcome. Speaking to you like this is my every-moment-life.
It is what I focus my energies upon.

Personal Story

I am a new mother and yet I have been feeling maternal for most of my life. Recently, I had my first child, a daughter, whom first spoke to me by telepathy on a wooded mountain in New Mexico. I heard her voice speak so very clearly. Ava, as we have come to name her, "informed" me that, "There will be two of us, first a girl and then a boy. We will be about three years apart and we are coming to you because you will understand and support our unique gifts."

Ever since that day I have understood that much is already in place, despite what my eyes could perceive. For example, I didn't know my children but my children knew me. This experience changed me and has caused me to recommit many times to stay in the place of "listening" while relating to my children. A place where my spirit can do the relating and then operate from this expanded communication. In this place of listening, I experience the spirit of our second, unborn child and commune with "him".

(con't on next page)

Please, breathe with us, so that you can know us thoroughly. My combination has surfaced (for humans) at times when you have needed me.

That is why I am known, again, upon the Earth, now.

I have been known at other times, other ages, when people took big leaps in growth and possibilities. I was with many in Atlantis. I urged the synergy of combining energies in ways that would encourage power and balance simultaneously.

I have been used for ritual, for manifestation, for visioning far beyond this world.

I wish to support you. I want to be with you as you explore your technologies perhaps as never before in the her/history of humans. Keep me nearby.

I will ground your bodies so that you remember the consequences of how you grow, of what you do.

Whenever you create something, you are utilizing energy that affects all beings upon this Earth Mother. Humans are not alone and they never have been.

Take heart! That means you can open your beings to greater possibilities than your technologies alone could offer you. Look around you!!!! You belong in and with a vast web of life that is ever intertwined and it will serve you, as you serve it. You can know friends and love and wisdom from all beings.

You do not have to THINK of everything.

This process would not be possible without the support of the stones. There have been too many to list in total, however, one day, Marilyn called to share that, quite without judgment and with great wonder, she purchased two Super Seven stones. I have a pretty extensive stone family but had not met this particular variety. They came to her at a high price for their tiny size but she said, "Yes!" all the same. Upon listening to them, she realized that these little beauties were the stones of my children, both born and not yet born. To this invitation, I responded with a resounding, "Yes!" also.

Each stone is very distinct and beautiful. I have yet to really understand how they relate to each child, this is for them to distinguish individually, but what I know is that when I hold that of my unborn child, I feel him more intimately. I speak to him and welcome him with my whole heart; whenever the timing of his birth is, is perfect.

This whole process creates great mystery for me and that is grand. Faith moves mountains. And the mountains I move are

(con't on next page)

Torbernite

I am a beautiful green Phosphate mineral, somewhat radioactive. I was named by a Swedish chemist, Torbern Bergman. I am found in granites and other uranium bearing deposits as a secondary mineral. My most common alternate names are Copper Uranite and Cuprouranite. I have some significance as an ore of Uranium and my wonderful color makes me attractive to collectors also. I am very soft and brittle and should be handled with care.

Emotional (Crystalline Grid) Bridge: I am full of never-ending explosions. Whatever fears and thrills come to you will move you on to another vista, another adventure.

Evolutionary Support: I am dangerously alive. I vibrate with the inner core of life. When you touch me (or connect with me), everything in you will quake with the fullest spectrum of light and sound.

Where you have blockages, they will want to break free. Listen to your body and to your whole story and they will guide you. They will hold you when you think you are alone with pain.

Where you have freedom, touching me will soar you into your finest dreams. Root yourself into yourself and then into the Earth, so that you can dance with the immensity of perfection.

Tools for Co-Creation

Sit upon the Earth.
Quiet in mind and in voice
gaze at everything.
Savor the colors, the songs and the free-traveling scents.
Now go more deeply into that
by journeying INTO the Earth.

within my own being. As a parent, I choose to offer my children a space that supports them being comfortable in their own skin, whatever that picture may look like. I don't know how to do that yet, but I have willingness to listen and operate from the most expanded parts of myself, where that experience is infinitely available. These Super Sevens support me in my commitment. They offer to teach me the things I don't yet consciously understand.

Such commitment as conscious parenting requires great support. Many challenging emotions and unresolved issues find me in the process of raising this little girl. Having the opportunity to expand further, safely, with the support of stones like the Seven's, brings me resolution eventually, always. The mystery of how to successfully parent consciously, from this expanded vantage point, is multifaceted and deeply personal. Mystery reigns and that which is private stays so until something sacred happens. My children's Super Sevens are perfect expressions of this.

~Cari W.

What are the different forms and ways of life there?
Can you learn to speak their languages wherever you are?

Personal Story

Every person on this planet has unique totem guides that speak right to their hearts (if they are listening). Many of you talk with your angels and nothing can touch that sweetly protective connection. For us, we walk and talk with nature Spirits. They bring out the innocent divinity in us that lies just below our human surface. You already know about the Stonefamilies that travel so generously with us, but there are more.......One of our most talkative, irrepressible guides has been a big, wide-open sprite named Turkll.

For years and years (probably lifetimes) we have talked with him when we have felt so desperate that not even a star could get us to look up. We have given him our hearts. He knows everything about us and because he inhabits multi-dimensions, he judges absolutely nothing and simply gives us the biggest pictures of life possible just when we need them. He doesn't sleep and he will come to us any time and any place we ask. To get anything in the universe he has to give, we just have to speak up: one question will do it. We asked him to give us a personal stone story for this book-adventure, and here it is for all of us:

Fossilized Palm Tree

Emotional (Crystalline Grid) Bridge: It slips into my hand and we know our creativity. We can point our intent in any direction.

Personal Story:

I love this Fossilized Palm Stone Wand. When I hold it, it calls me to the Earth and I land upon home. I can feel all the stories of all the beings here come alive, like an action video with unlimited plot lines.

Together with this Stone, I offer pure acceptance for every story and every event. And we root it right into the Earth, so that when you need anything, it is waiting for you. It always waits for you. If you ask for it, right now, it will come to you and fill you with impossible wonder...except that it won't be impossible any more!

Thanks for asking for my story.

~Turkll

Vesuvianite

I am a green, brown, yellow or blue Silicate mineral and probably most often seen in my green form. I was first found close by lavas on Mount Vesuvius, hence my name. My bluish form is known as Cyprine and has been found in Franklin, New Jersey and other places. The blue color is due to impurities of Copper. Californite is a name for me when I appear as a Jade-like variety. When I am rich in Manganese, I am called Xanthite. I am called Wiluite in my variety from Siberia. In the past I have also been called Idocrase as a gemstone.

Emotional (Crystalline Grid) Bridge: While you are listening to Stones (or learning that fine art), listen powerfully, gently, freely, innocently, to your heart. It aches to be heard by your fullness. I sit with it and I love its unique beauty. Have you known it yet?

Evolutionary Support: Breathe. Drink in my essence. I can be very grounded or very ethereal with you. I change according to what's around me.

Bring me your requests. There is no end to how we might come together............

Tools for Co-Creation

Use me in your meditations.
Hold me. Together we will make them as fleshed as suits you.
We can land your visions upon the Earth.
Or if you prefer we'll keep breeding them in the Sky
until you are ready to live them
to breathe them
here.

This 5 foot tall Gold Buddha links us to the wisdom of all parts of the Earth and all its dimensions. He happily resides in the home of one of the Freedom Intent participants.

Whisperings......

A dream visited us...........so many friends came up to us and smiled, hugged us. Some even shook our hands. Their grins beamed into us from the top of our heads to the bottoms of our roots.

Everyone got hugged. Everything. The Earth, the friends, the smiles.

The friends are part of us, as much as arms, legs, and breaths. We are so intertwined, so beautiful in our circle. How lovely-lovely-loving to touch each other......because they don't "live" here, they live in other places, other dimensions. Yet they live within us and even around us when we listen, when we throw ourselves off the cliffs of change, trusting with eyes and hearts fully open.

Can you cry in dreams?

Looking for their faces in the wide-awake-world, too.

We're here.

Stone Combination Section

Aphrodite

- **Rhodochrosite** — I move and grow with lifeforce and it brings more lifeforce!
- **Herkimer Diamond** — I look at all things from all directions until beauty smiles at me —
- **Peridot** — I always open the heart, through your freedom.

Physical, Emotional, Mental Integration: We land upon the doorway of your heart and offer it the most loving, beautiful bouquets of simple life.

Electrical Body Alignment: We link you to the utter loveliness of being.

Affirmation of Support: *"I am beauty in every way, in every act."*

Tools for Manifestation

Hold us to your heart.

Now look into a mirror. Find the beauty there and say it aloud!

Keep looking into the mirror until you find what you believe is ugliness.

Keep looking and watching and seeing how it moves and grows.

Look through our eyes

until you find beauty in every part of you that you can possibly affirm.

Say it aloud!

Do this at least once every day until you find the beauty in yourself automatically.

Yes!

Complementary Tools

When you wish to expand even further, join this combination with:

"Venus"— This Act of Power Planetary Wand potently urges you to expand your intent from your body to your resonant field, to all your acts, with beauty and grace.

"Bountiful Harvest"— During days of great ritual (like holidays), place your "Aphrodite" combination next to this House as Teacher combination to attract the pure, open-hearted abundance of all life to you and to your space.

"Transformation, Prosperity and the Goddess"— Spray yourself with this Stonessence (while wearing "Aphrodite") while walking in nature to heighten all your senses, including your profound appreciation.

Business Success

- **Alaskan Magnetite** — I connect you with the Earth Mother and vast reserves of vitality and stability.
- **Red Garnet** — I align you with the source of your creativity, bliss and productivity.
- **Sunstone** — I catalyze into action your unique leadership qualities.

Physical, Emotional, Mental Integration: We help align all parts of your being— especially body, heart, mind and spirit— until they flow with one, smiling creativity. Then when you meet challenge, you have all your resources at the ready, and when you work with others, you apply this same ease, spontaneously and immediately.

Electrical Body Alignment: We link you to bringing your Spirit into your everyday reality each moment, now.

Affirmation of Support: *"I work and create with Spirit!"*

Tools for Manifestation

We welcome you to manifesting with us. It is our joy. It is our gift.

Wear us constantly and most of all, wear us when you are working.

Just get used to feeling us (during your work) without words.

Let us freely fill you with new life and new possibilities.

Open yourself to all of it.

This is how you work and play and live in ever new ways.

Open yourself to all of it.

Disease into Vitality: Addiction Support

- **Ruby** — I offer you utter appreciation of your perfect body and ever-growing lifeforce.
- **Malachite** — I link the heart and the body with all the other parts of your being as if they have never been separate.
- **Pyrite** — Look around you! All you see is a treasure and you can experience it all as you wish.
- **Moonstone** — I embrace all emotions, equally, unconditionally.

Physical, Emotional, Mental Integration: We offer you the remembrance that all is perfect, that everything exists in divine order, including every single part of you. We reinvigorate your body while soothing your mind and uniting you with all of life, lovingly.

Electrical Body Alignment: I link you with your soul's choice to be here and to experience all things in love.

Affirmation of Support: "I AM acceptance."

Tools for Manifestation

Right now is the only moment that truly exists.

Our freedom gives us the choice to accept that and live that completely

or not.

Accept it.

Live right now.

Just live right now.

Hold this combination while you make your choice

and announce the Affirmation of Support
with all your heart and all your being.
As you hold the combination, let every part of yourself
come together
right now,
this moment
and live utterly.

Disease into Vitality: Adrenal Support

- **Rutile** — You like energy, well here it is— connected to lifeforce and peace at once.
- **Blue Lace Agate** — I show all the softness and sweetness of life unfolding around you and simultaneously within you.
- **Iolite** — Let's join with the biggest picture of life where you are divine and free of the illusion of fear and struggle.
- **Amblygonite** — You are a powerful being who can choose to focus on anything you wish, and you do this exactly, whether you realize it or not.

Physical, Emotional, Mental Integration: Relax.

Electrical Body Alignment: We link you with the innocence of being.

Affirmation of Support: *"Life is kind and I welcome it, calmly."*

Tools for Manifestation

Every time you feel stress rising uncomfortably within you,

stop everything possible.

Breathe.

Inhale so fully that you fill your body with peace.

Consciously, clearly see yourself fill each individual part of your body

with peace that makes every toe, every eyelash, every cell

grin.

Say out loud: Life is kind and I welcome it, calmly.

Smile again at the wonder of it.

Now smile at every part of your body that you can

with great joy and appreciation for their constant work for you in growing calm.

Do this each time stress seems to be overtaking your innate, true peace.

Complementary Tools

When you wish to expand even further, join this combination with:

"Disease into Vitality: Adrenal Support Wand"— In our rush-rush society, our adrenal glands bear much of the over-burdening of our bodies and minds. We have found that wearing the Vibrational Jewelry "Adrenal Support" necklace, while using the same combination in the Act of Power Wand and in the Stonessence—all simultaneously—offers tremendously exponential relief, right away.

Using the different forms of the same Stonecombination focuses your intent consciously and clearly on exactly what you choose. With so much focus working for you, there's less space *for* distractions and resistance to work **against** you.

Disease into Vitality: Back Support

- **Tourmaline** — I anchor you into the peace of the Earth Mother, now, and now.
- **Hematite** — I connect your actions with your Spirit.
- **Peridot** — I face your greatest challenges, with you, and together we discover they are your finest strengths and treasures.
- **Silver** — I stand your spine, strong, because it aligns firmly and easily this way: It allows you to feel life, so that it can feed you as you most need.

Physical, Emotional, Mental Integration: We know that just being alive can seem utterly difficult. We join with you in this and as you feel challenge, we accept it unconditionally. Whether you realize it consciously or not, you feel our acceptance filling you and letting go of the difficulty (as you wish), until you straighten up and can face anything freely.

Electrical Body Alignment: We align you with natural courage and stamina.

Affirmation of Support: *"I embrace life, just as it is, with freedom and joy!"*

Tools for Manifestation

Your body is a pure gift.

It is a treasure that allows the preciousness of Spirit

to walk

to see

to hear

Personal Story

When Q, my dog and soul mate of almost 15 years died, I decided to try the "Death" pendant to help me with my grief. I thought I had made great strides in healing from his transition, but as I opened the box and held the beautiful pendant for the first time, I could feel just how much I was still hanging onto him. With this realization I "let go" of him at that moment and a great peace swept over me and a love so unconditional completely embraced me. It was very beautiful and profound.

~Linda T.

to cry

to bleed

to breathe.

Every day, hold us.

Then truly savor one thing that your body simply gives you.

Revel in that gift all day long.

When you have a quiet moment, remember the gift!

Celebrate it.

Hold it high above all your struggle so that you can see this more clearly and delightedly than anything else.

Carry your gift into life and see how it leads you.

Disease into Vitality: Brain Support

- **Madagascar Phenakite** — Be utterly present with your body, a point of power and peace.
- **Smithsonite** — Absorb the world. Whatever you need comes to you.
- **Hemimorphite** — Change continually. Let life guide you through your life.
- **AquaPhenakite** — Be utterly present with your Spirit, the point of power and peace.

Physical, Emotional, Mental Integration: When we decide that we know everything (when we are controlling everything), we give away the freedom that we inherently are. Your brain links you to truth and divine intelligence when you are free and act upon your own freedom. Yes.

Electrical Body Alignment: We join you with every inspiration possible and impossible.

Affirmation of Support: *"I act upon my own, divine spark of genius!"*

Tools for Manifestation

You are human.

You are divine.

These exist simultaneously and perfectly within you.

If you cannot understand that, it is because your mind-alone dominates you.

Free yourself.

Relax.

Meditate.

Let go of words.

In the soft, sweet stillness between thoughts,

in the space between the words,

in the silence between the breaths

in the void between the worlds

lives truth.

It is you.

It is simply you.

It will go out into the world and create unthought-of miracles.

Disease into Vitality: Chakra Support

- **Wolframite** — I bring you to your body—your reality—to respond.
- **Carnelian** — I help you find the resources to fulfill dreams.
- **Amblygonite** — I stand in truth and love and reflect that in all realities, endlessly.
- **Kornerupine** — I warm the heart knowing that it leads the body and the mind.
- **Blue Apatite** — I point out the truth confidently, innocently, joyfully.
- **Amethyst** — I share the wonder of it all!
- **Pakistani "Herkimer" Diamond** — I focus on consciousness, hone awareness, and release everything else.

Physical, Emotional, Mental Integration: We warm every part of your body and fill you with lifeforce. We thrill to the passion within you, knowing that all this energy inspires you and grows your dreams. Your body is home.

Electrical Body Alignment: We unite you with all of life happening at once, in perfect divine order.

Affirmation of Support: "I AM utterly alive!"

Tools for Manifestation

As inspiration comes to you,

write down whatever truly enflames you.

Smile.

Keep writing down each thing, simply and clearly.

Smile.

Write without editing or judgment. Let inspiration take you over!

Smile.

Just do this quietly and simply whenever your kind dreams land upon you.

One day when you feel alone and lost,

take out your inspirations and read them

until you smile again.

You are home.

Disease into Vitality: Kidney Support

- **Dravite** — is peace. It's peaceful absolutely inhabiting your body and supporting your Spirit with all your presence.
- **Hematite** — soothes the blood and cools impatience.
- **Rutilated Quartz** — talks with all parts of your body and being, joining all.
- **Citrine** — uplifts you where you most need it.

Physical, Emotional, Mental Integration: We give you a strong foundation for everything, so that you can give and receive in great abundance and bliss. We remind you: You are connected to everything and this is your most amazing challenge and power.

Electrical Body Alignment: We join you with the taking in of life and spontaneously releasing it freely and utterly gracefully.

Affirmation of Support: *"I am lovingly and joyfully connected with life!"*

Tools for Manifestation

When you read these words,

take them into your body.

Give them a home.

Let them land wherever they wish to be;

do not direct them.

Let them breathe with your kidneys,

or your ears

or the soles of your feet.

Each day

each moment

each breath

it will be different.

The gifts of these Stonebeings will balance with you,

wherever your body most needs them.

Live that balance.

Feel it wherever it lands.

Be that free.

Disease into Vitality: Liver Support

- **Phenakite** — I root you into the Earth Mother, so that you can release all struggle and pain.
- **Zoisite** — I bring you joy to share!
- **Kyanite** — All around you live the Guardian Spirits who protect you and love you beyond yourself: See them. Feel them.
- **White Moldavite** — I bring you face to face with all change, for this is the face of Life.

Physical, Emotional, Mental Integration: We support the biggest organ of your body, so we simultaneously support your biggest visions. Breathe with us. Release unneeded blockages. Free yourself into the dreams that you came here to be, to breathe, to walk.

Electrical Body Alignment: We join you with the peace beneath the fire of your passions and inspirations dancing freely.

Affirmation of Support: "I see my dreams and I give them to life!"

Tools for Manifestation

Hold us upon your liver.

There is no need to understand this.

Set yourself free of any expectations.

Now dream.

See your own field of dreams.

Let it be a place that utterly welcomes you.

Come back to it over and over again.

Change it whenever and however you wish.

It is yours to birth more creativity

for the biggest pictures of your life.

Complementary Tools

When you wish to expand even further, join this combination with:

"Jupiter"— This Act of Power Planetary Wand innately relates to the liver and urges you to release overpowering, unhelpful emotions now.

"Environmental Toxins"— This Stonessence supports your liver being so strong that it can keep releasing toxins as long as needed.

Disease into Vitality: Lymph Support

- **Rutile** — I awaken the Lifeforce in all parts of you.
- **Sunstone** — I encourage you to change with the flow of love and life.
- **Green Tourmaline** — I open your heart to all possibilities until you embrace every experience as golden.
- **Hemimorphite** — I integrate all of your meridians and all of your polarities until you become one with all that you are and can be.

Physical, Emotional, Mental Integration: We move life and energy through, even when your resistance slows things. We help you to truly feel your emotions so that you can release them freely when they are done.

Electrical Body Alignment: We unite you with the constancy of flow and movement.

Affirmation of Support: *"I love changing with the flow of life."*

Tools for Manifestation

Each day hug this combination to your heart.

Fill yourself with the constant ever-flowing rhythms of life.

Move. Dance. Stretch.

Then make a list of changes that you are welcoming into your life now.

At the end of the week, look over your list and see how you have transformed

and how you have not......so that you can welcome in more change (as you wish) and integrate how you have grown.

Complementary Tools

When you wish to expand even further, join this combination with:

"Clear Space" — a vibrational essence that keeps the energy ever moving and enlivened within you, and within your space, which will then lovingly support who you are and what you are becoming, simultaneously.

"Alchemy" — an Act of Power Wand that moves you beyond resistance into the full co-creatorship that awaits you......all according to your own freedom.

"Perfect Release" — a House as Teacher Stonecombination to support you continually, constantly releasing whatever you no longer need in a kind, compassionate way.

Disease into Vitality: Nasal and Sinus Support

- **Himalayan Black Tourmaline (from above 20,000 feet) —** I take you to the core of your healing with all of your body and being.
- **Peridot** — I open your heart to unknown love.
- **Malachite** — I align your body with your heart.
- **Alpine Pollucite** — I connect your breathing with your Spirit.

Physical, Emotional, Mental Integration: You are loved and accepted by your Spirit, just as you are, right here and right now. Take that feeling (not the replaying of your old, unneeded experiences) into your health and into your vitality, now.

Electrical Body Alignment: We join you with cellular memory and perfection.

Affirmation of Support: *"I live now. I revel in perfection right now!"*

Tools for Manifestation

Breathe with us.

Just breathe with us.

Let go of ideas.

Let go of anything you "have" to do.

Just breathe and feel whatever comes to you.

Sometimes when you focus on healing,

it inadvertently tells your old beliefs that something is wrong with you.

Everything is well.

All is perfect.

Breathe that.

Breathe.

Complementary Tools

When you wish to expand even further, join this combination with:

"Air"— This Elemental Wand embraces the element of air all around you and within you simultaneously. With it, you drink in—you feast!—upon the full loveliness of air in every inhale and every exhale.

"Air"— This Elemental Essence soothes everything in your body and helps each part of you to digest air according to the very unique, moment-to-moment needs of each part of your body and being.

Hawk's Wish

- **Hawkseye Velvet Tourmaline** — I reach across time, space, and dreams to witness your perfection on all levels.
- **Hematite** — I circulate blood and strength to wherever you need it.
- **Falcon's Eye** — I invite us to unite physical and Sacred Witness vision.
- **Nepalese Quartz** — I continually ask you to focus on perfection— to embrace it within you.

Physical, Emotional, Mental Integration: Welcome regeneration, refreshment and vigor on all levels! We support stress coming and going from the body and mind freely. Let that clarity transform your being. We encourage you to claim your power and expand your creativity: See your world as you choose, now.

Electrical Body Alignment: We link you with vision and visions.

Affirmation of Support: *"Everything I see brings me wisdom!"*

Tools for Manifestation

Remember: what you see and the visions that you have,

come from the core of your being.

They live and breathe and grow from the same place.

If you look around and cannot focus easily,

stop.

Breathe.

Know yourself.

Accept everything.

Personal Story

Dearest Marilyn,

It has been too many days and I have not yet written to let you know that I received my profound and totally wonderful custom necklace. I laughed with joy as I read its description. It is indeed perfect for me in this now moment and more than likely way beyond. My heartfelt thanks to you and Tohmas for such a perfectly amazing gift.

The divinely spiritual and powerful energy of it and my Unimaginability (the name of the Stonecombination) started to be felt in just two days. My life has indeed opened up in new and amazing ways. They are working together so seamlessly, each enhancing the gift and mission of the other exponentially.

My life has already started to bring forth and manifest deep and abiding blessings that I not only would not have thought of, but if such thoughts had come to mind, I would most likely have dismissed them as impossible, or as my mind playing tricks on

(con't on next page)

Your visions want to join with your vision.
How can your reality and dreams join
to create your honest, respectful life?

me, thus closing the door on or rejecting the marvels that the Divine universe has in store for me. "I AM all that is; may we be who we are, the light that is."

Love,

Aranyah

Integrating the Mental Body

- **Arizona Hematite** — roots you into yourself so that you integrate everything and utterly immerse yourself in the bounty of life.
- **Brazilian Blue Apatite** — offers joy and peace, simultaneously, so that any worries are simply not needed.
- **Hawaiian Calcite** — balances everything continually.
- **Russian Phenacite** — unites you with your soul, though you have never been apart.
- **Pakistan "Herkimer" Diamond with Anatase/Brookite influence** — clarifies your visions and dreams so that you can create their reality now.
- **Moroccan Fulgurite** — helpfully interrupts your old, unneeded habits and patterns.

Physical, Emotional, Mental Integration: Let go of monkey mind. Whenever any one sense (or part of you) makes most of your decisions, you are out of balance. Come back into balance; find out what else life has to offer beyond your safe, decaying habits. Free yourself to merge with the cosmic mind.

Electrical Body Alignment: We remind you to join with cosmic intelligence.

Affirmation of Support: *"I AM part of all wisdom!"*

Tools for Manifestation

How many ways can you experience life

without letting thinking completely define you and the world?

Breathe.

Let air soften and unfold your body.

Dance.

Soar into the air <u>and</u> touch the ground.

Caress.

Hug someone you love without need, without explanation.

Smell.

Stand in a field of flowers. Let the aromas talk to you in their own rich petals.

Taste.

Eat nothing. Let your body unclench. When you feel free, savor your favorite food,

slowly,

softly,

swimmingly.

You are fueling life.

Your unworded senses set you free.

Kwan Yin

- **Ruby** — thrills you to the core, where you know fearlessly, that you are an utterly magnificent creation.
- **Gold** — warms all your blockages until inspired creativity flows out of every wondrous part of you!
- **Silver** — kindly coaxes you to listen to all parts of life so that all you do honors everything.
- **Burmese Phenakite** — loves all, smoothes all, integrates all.

Physical, Emotional, Mental Integration: This combination brings the most unimaginably compassionate Being-within to every part of your reality. Ah!

Electrical Body Alignment: We link you to your Divine Mother.

Affirmation of Support: ***"I nurture myself with complete freedom and delight~"***

Tools for Manifestation

Sit quietly.

Close your eyes.

Let thoughts melt into nothingness.

Shrug your shoulders.

Shake off your worries.

Drop your weight gently into the Earth.

Let her carry you completely and effortlessly.

She rocks you within her arms and her skies.

Ask your cells to take you back to a single moment

when you felt utterly cared for and carefree.

Savor it.

Send the feeling of that moment to every single part of you.

Let it fill your cup until it overflows.

Now go out into the world

and share the feeling.

LifeBlood

- **Red Jasper with Pyrite** — This is a time of great excitement and I help you to meet it with great readiness and fortune.
- **Vanadinite** — Let us connect with your core creativity. What can you not respond to then?
- **Red Zincite** — I bring to this Stonecombination, and to you, the timeless wisdom of your beautiful en-spirited body.
- **Herkimer Diamond** — I offer vision and joy to the tremendous power and sheer energy that the other Stonebeings bring here.

Physical, Emotional, Mental Integration: This is a time of tremendous evolution for this planet and its beings. We Stones know of this and we offer our fullest services to all of our co-evolutionaries. This combination will continually and insistently present you with utter energy, for you will need that to face every fear and every separation— to be union— to be whole beings. Wearing us will help you to see that most of your human-reality needs will not ready you for this evolution. We remind you of the core priorities and how acting upon them will fill you with the energy that you need and has ever been available to you......but was momentarily hidden by fear.

Electrical Body Alignment: We connect you with all the energy that your body was designed to hold and to use well.

Affirmation of Support: *"I am alive with the passion for life."*

Tools for Manifestation

You believe that many things keep you alive: food, drink, sleep, warmth and so on.

Yet do you know what keeps you truly alive and thriving?

Can you know that when the stimuli of society speak so loudly and so continually?

When you first receive this Stonecombination,

take at least an entire day and go into the quiet.

If you can, go out onto the land:

Fast, Listen and Be still, inside and out.

What does Life tell you then?

We are partners with Life and we bring her wisdom directly to you.

We help you to translate her pure energy into the words that you so love.

Listen. Listen until you absolutely KNOW what makes you truly live.

Listening to Animals

- **Snowflake Obsidian** — Together we witness the miracle of life, letting go of judgment.
- **Sodalite** — I offer you the truth, freely and simply.
- **Hawkseye Velvet Tourmaline** — I shift your attachment to linear time and space, so that you can meet Animals in the heart.........
- **Selenite** — I bring you empathy for all things, in all ways, in all moments.

Physical, Emotional and Mental Integration: We bring you to the core where you live and breathe as one with all beings upon the Earth. Hold us next to your heart and it will find unconditional acceptance for everything, especially Animals.

Electrical Body Alignment: We link you with your Animal self.

Affirmation of Support: *"I listen to and empathize with all Animals, now."*

Tools for Manifestation

When you receive this combination, consciously hold it to your heart.

Ask to listen to the Animals around you.

Ask specifically if there is an Animal Totem Spirit that can guide you to communicating with all Animals, unconditionally.

Wait.

Breathe.

Accept the messages you receive.

Live the wisdom.

Living in Vulnerability

- **Tasmanian Crocoite** — I show you what it is to be fragile in form, and strong in Spirit.
- **Lithium Crystal** — Together we balance your body, mind and heart, as they need it, when they need it.
- **South African Petalite** — Hello! I inspire you. I point out the soft and incredible wonders of the world that whisper of the magnificence of every life form.
- **Fuschite** — I bring you to adventure in a gentle AND excited way so that you can learn to revel in any experience, any time—no matter what it is.
- **Amblygonite** — I fill your aura gently, to insistently remind you of your own beautiful power, over and over, again.

Physical, Emotional, Mental Integration: Today is your life. Together we walk through it and experience it ALL, though we know that some of it will feel tough. We open our hearts fully, knowing that love will show us unexpected wisdom in every moment that we allow it. We will help you to quiet your mind so that you can keep hearing your heart always, in everything.

Electrical Body Alignment: We link you with your ever opening heart and your innocent inner child.

Affirmation of Support: *"I am peace in all that I do and be."*

Tools for Manifestation

Welcome.

Living in Vulnerability may sound scary to you, right?

It can call up images of you not being as graceful or as connected as you would always like to be.

Consciously draw up each of those images.

Examine them clearly, one by one.

As you view them, ask yourself, "What am I really afraid of?"

Keep asking yourself until you find out everything that scares you about your own vulnerability.

Then face each of those fears, one by one.

Learn from them.

Be grateful for them, and let them go.

Mother Earth

- **Mexican Fire Opal** — I ask you to come more deeply into the Earth Mother where she offers you all her love unconditionally. Feel how you belong here perfectly.
- **Colorado AquaPhenakite** — I show us new life all around so we can revel in that fresh inspiration any time we allow it.
- **Brazilian Anatase** — I help us to focus upon knowing we are on the Earth no matter what and assist us in creating our own path of beauty here!
- **Russian Phenakite** — I show us that when we are fully rooted in the Earth we can soar and no dreams are beyond our reach.
- **Una Oportunidad Sagrada Stonessence** — combines with these Stonebeings to help you find your absolutely unique and personal union with the Earth Mother.

Physical, Emotional, Mental Integration: Welcome home. All Stonebeings are here, welcoming you home, as you wish, as you allow. In this moment, we combine to speak that loudly enough so that you can hear us above your ancient defenses and illusions. We offer our hearts to you fully. We invite you to join us in feelings (not thoughts) where understanding comes but only when you have surrendered yourself to trust.

Electrical Body Alignment: We link you with accepting the Earth as your home.

Affirmation of Support: *"I am cared for and belong upon the Earth Mother."*

Tools for Manifestation

Every moment you are alive, you are upon the Earth Mother.

You might forget this because she seems to hide under cement and asphalt,

but she is always here.

Speak with her.

Listen with her.

Ask her how you can grow your relationship with her so that you know you are at home.

Ask her how you can grow your relationship with her to show her your gratitude.

If you forget that you are always walking on the Earth Mother,

carry our words with you.

We will remind you from the core of love—the heart of the Earth Mother.

New Prosperity

- **Pyrite** — I place you into your bodies and your lives for full-conscious-JOY!
- **Carnelian** — I inspire us to focus on ever unlimited dreams.
- **Amblygonite** — I inspire divine order from chaos.
- **Green Apatite** — I empower us to accept the gift in each experience.

Physical, Emotional, Mental Integration: We encourage you to accept your full worth. Wear it, walk it, smile it. Celebrate your individuality, within the whole. Remember to give and to receive from the bounty of all life. This is your birthright and you have read it, consciously, now, so that you can embody it, again and again.

Electrical Body Alignment: We link you with prosperity in the New Earth paradigm.

Affirmation of Support: *"I AM provided for endlessly and perfectly."*

Tools for Manifestation

Throughout the ages of humans,

you have known prosperity in different ways.

In some times

it has meant being able to run freely

or finding a buffalo to feed a tribe

or birthing a healthy child.

In all times,

it means remembering what you love—

reveling in all the forms of love that have ever visited you.

Prosperity seems to change as humans change.

So let your feelings of prosperity change until you satisfy yourself with

the endless bounty of what you already have

and of whom you already are.

Star Offerings

- **Tibetan Tektite** — I offer you universal channels of communication with respect.
- **Chrysocolla** — I offer you the kindness of Earth.
- **Turquoise** — I continually show you how to find your ever deeper truth.
- **Calcite** — I align us to our ever-evolving selves and splendor.

Physical, Emotional, Mental Integration: Hello~ When we are with you (as you wish) we gently ground your body, calm your mind and encourage your Spirit. This deepens our appreciation for the Earth; it insists upon our constant, full presence while expanding our precious compassion. Thank you.

Electrical Body Alignment: We link you to the universe. Ho!

Affirmation of Support: *"Wherever my Spirit sings, I am home."*

Tools for Manifestation

In the Universe, there is room and respect enough for all beings of love.

There are endless Stars, Planets, Suns and mysteries.

They are part of us

wherever we are

whomever we are.

Even if we don't remember this,

it is so.

When we look out beyond ourselves,

we look to the Stars.

We look to where we don't already understand

to be more

complete.

Hold us whenever you look upon the Stars.

Feel the longing and the satisfaction together.

Complementary Tools

When you wish to expand even further, join this combination with:

"Act of Power Planetary Wand Set"— These Wands bring forth the unconditional, archetypal energy of the planets into your life. Each one emphasizes a core learning while you adventure on Planet Earth.

"Space Merkabah"— This Stonessence ever reminds you that there is always a bigger picture to look at and to join for your own peace and evolution.

SUPER HEROES! . . . .
Astral Travel

(Astral travel is an ancient art where people took their consciousness out into the world, without being limited by their physical bodies.)

- **Phenacite** — I align with all respectful realities, right now.
- **Lapis Lazuli** — Here is ancient, timeless wisdom that has integrated seamlessly with humans and is further evolving with them now.
- **Moonstone** — I guide you in all your travels. I welcome you wherever you land.
- **Aquamarine** — Welcome. I urge you to think and act with such newness that you enlighten yourself right now.

Physical, Emotional, Mental Integration: Here and now: We so welcome you to this exact moment, in which you can do anything. When you do anything, you also will be anything.

Electrical Body Alignment: We join you with real magic.

Affirmation of Support: *"I can go anywhere safely, happily and consciously."*

Tools for Manifestation

We, Stonebeings,
have come together to support you
in a miracle that you can do and
that you already are.
Please keep us nearby.
Chant into us constantly.
Chant the most amazing intents and Ohms—
the ones that soar your soul!
Create affirmations so freeing that you sigh and giggle just committing them to paper and to saying them out loud.
Say them all day long.

Personal Story

About our newest line of Stonecombinations: Super Hero Support!

Yes yes yes! Oh my yes!

When we were listening to and birthing this beautiful heart-book, it landed upon us like a miracle—a rainbow in spotless sunlight. It twisted and spiraled us so that we could look at life from angles that never existed before. We could see, we could see! the new world that our dreams had hinted about always: it breathes. It is alive.

Watching the miracle gives AND takes so much energy to digest it. Imagine us dancing as fast as we can on the tippy-top of the world. By sunset, we set, too: exhausted, exhilarated, confused, awed and frustrated—all things at once.

Just when we thought that implosion was imminent . . . a little Stone whisper slipped out . . . (so that it wouldn't scare us) and it spoke softly, "You are Super Heroes; we'll show you. We'll give you a new line of Stonecombinations to bring

(con't on next page)

Say them as you are falling asleep at night when your body and soul prepare for a different reality and different kinds of travel.
Nothing can stop you when you focus on creating any reality that is born of respect and Freedom.

out the Super hero in you. It's who you are and everything you are doing is simply another step towards complete acceptance of the amazing abilities that you already are. You are bringing reality to all your dreams. They live inside of you—carefully set aside in your DNA and in your cells until you are ready to wear them gracefully. That moment has arrived. Your species is evolving and you will do and be things that make imagination real."

Of course. What a glorious, magnificent gift! We accept, we accept!!!

Dear Everyone,

As we all stretch ourselves through our greatest difficulties and thrills, help is here. It is within us. It has been breeding in all of us all along and now there is support to bring out all these resources and marvels, just when we most need them.

These combinations contain special, specific and unique stones. Not just an Aquamarine for instance, but THE Aquamarine that holds the energy called out for by this special combination. It takes a lot of extra effort and

(con't on next page)

SUPER HEROES! ....
Bi-location

(Bi-location is the ancient art of physically being in more than one place at the same time. Ho!)

- **Basalt** — Ground into me, so that you can know everything so well that you know how to respectfully, immediately, and powerfully utilize everything available to you.
- **Apache Tear** — I protect you so easily that you fearlessly become all that you are.
- **Realgar** — With me, you know pure alchemy—a magic beyond dreams, landing into reality.
- **Fuschite** — I give you strength, in flexibility, innocence, and the peace to detach from everything now.

Physical, Emotional, Mental Integration: Like us, you are a crystal. Your facets shine in many worlds as one. For ages, we have witnessed you and how you travel through lives upon lives. Open up our libraries. See how the possible has always merged with the impossible and be that merging. Be possible with your impossibilities, just as we are.

Electrical Body Alignment: We join you with the pure miraculousness of all life.

Affirmation of Support: *"I am here. I am everywhere at once."*

Tools for Manifestation

Keep us next to your bed.
Before you go to sleep each night, say the above Affirmation of Support,
"I am here. I am everywhere at once."
Together we will stretch your reality and imprint you with ever increasing possibilities.
Immediately upon awaking in the morning, clasp us to your heart.
Say the Affirmation of Support several times.

focus to ground these energies, so it takes special Stonebeings willing to offer themselves as well.

If you look to co-create these combinations for yourself, make sure you invest in the patience and honesty to find just the right Stones to join you on this journey. Your heart will know.

~Marilyn and Tohmas T.

When you feel its power spread to all parts of your being, announce to yourself, "It is so," or whatever statements allow you to co-create new reality with us now.
We witness it. We record it just as you announce it.
We record how strongly you mean what you say, and this is what registers in the Crystalline Grid for all.
It is what imprints this reality and keeps growing just as you keep intending.
It is so.

SUPER HEROES! ....
Limb Regeneration

(In many different times and places, people have been able to easily re-grow teeth; to re-grow bones; and to spontaneously heal in unbelievable ways. We dedicate this Stonecombination to the lizard in all of us.)

- **Sodalite** — I impress you with the purity of the truth landed upon your reality right here, right now.
- **Aegrine** — I stretch open your heart and your possibilities, simultaneously.
- **Hemimorphite** — Let's open up all your resources, all your divinity, for your conscious use.
- **Amblygonite** — Smile! For the world to change, all you have to do is bring in more possibilities than impossibilities.

Physical, Emotional, Mental Integration: Yipppppeeee! Everything in your body can regenerate completely with a little time and lots of intent. Use the alchemy of these Stones to grow your body anew, as you wish.

Electrical Body Alignment: We link you to your original, perfect blueprint of life.

Affirmation of Support: *"I can grow my body new, now!!!"*

Tools for Manifestation

Yes!
You can dream as big as you want.
Even though you will not always get what you expect, if you stay with your trust, you will get more!
Hold us with you every day.
Simultaneously talk with your body every day.
Ask it to help you. Ask it to truly blossom, to unfold miracles.
Tell it you are finally ready to honor all of your choices
and that will be the fuel for your newness.

Keep asking.
Keep intending.
Keep regenerating.

SUPER HEROES! . . . .
Super Power for You

(This is the MysteryCombination. What do YOU need? What power do you want to call to you because you can now wield it superbly and graciously? You name it. You put your own name on this Stonecombination; it will transmute to every honoring wish that lands upon it. Land yours now.)

- **Garnet** — I root you into your fullness and call upon your power in love.
- **Hematite** — I clear and re-charge your blood.
- **Malachite** — I worship your heart and I affirm the beauty of your blood, bones, and body.
- **Apophyllite** — I call in other loving dimensions and all your sweet guides.

Physical, Emotional, Mental Integration: You are an extraordinary being in extraordinary times. You are calling to you extraordinary power and support, yet it is also ordinary too, because power has always been in your full, core composition. It is up to you whether you will use it or not. We are here to remind you of compassion-in-strength.

Electrical Body Alignment: We link you to the most potent evolution you can allow.

Affirmation of Support: *"I am strong with unlimited lifeforce!"*

Tools for Manifestation

Bring us with you when you move your body.
Feel your muscles and nerves as they synchronize perfectly.
Stretch them. Reach them. Leap them. Spin them.
Listen to them.
Use them in unimaginable ways when your instincts shout, "NOW!"
Do this as often as you can and find as many different ways to experience your body's inherent perfection and strength as possible.
We will witness it and ever record your potentials and your constant

evolution.
You are a dream-in-progress.

Carry us with you in specific situations where you will need more reserves of power.
Our cellular memories will link with yours and activate you.
You will be more than you ever knew how to be.
It is your birthright.

SUPER HEROES! ....
Time Travel

(Who hasn't wanted to travel into the past and into the future and then live with them all in the present? Those of us on the planet, now, are living in the time of "no-time." Just ask any Mayan......It is our time to bend time, to let it reach out into its fullest beingness and not be held back by our old rules anymore.)

- **Nepalese High Altitude Tourmaline** — I stand with you in the most incredible, inspiring realities ever born and still being born.
- **Hawkseye Velvet Tourmaline** — I care for you so you are strong enough to shift all your vistas instantly and profoundly.
- **Violet-Blue Quartz** — Together we fill up the holes in you—the unsatisfied needs—so that you are free to go wherever you wish with joy.
- **Desert Snow Quartz** — Here come your most empowering guides. They whisper their all into your shaman's heart, now.

Physical, Emotional, Mental Integration: When you join with us, you truly realize how exquisite your full power is and can become.........We utterly appreciate how you are transforming and we bring that into your present, now. Feel it. We imprint it upon your former knowledge and all is changed.

Electrical Body Alignment: We fill you with utter imagination.

Affirmation of Support: *"I am a multi-dimensional being!"*

Tools for Manifestation

Wear us continually.
Observe the nature of time.
Watch how long it takes you to do anything
and see how much joy you do, or don't, bring to your tasks.

Constantly witness how the quality, and even the quantity, of time changes according to your presence.
How do you affect time? How does your consciousness change its voice?
Watch yourself: How do you feel about time? How do you speak of it? Do you listen to it? Do you join with it freely or stressfully?
Make friends with time.
Ask it to take you on travels that seemed impossible to you before Now.

Sweet Shield

- **Apache Tear** — encourages the feelings of others to pass through us freely, empowering us to be our own, loving selves.
- **Snowflake Obsidian** — reminds us to offer love to all, whether we understand them or not.
- **Lapis Lazuli** — calls upon the wisdom of the elders into our hearts and our intuition.
- **Phenakite** — embraces the sacredness of being, now.

Physical, Emotional, Mental Integration: Hello, I am Grandmother Sweet Shield. I have been two-legged and yet I am in, and with, these Stonebeings. So are you. We meet there—that is how we can talk and listen, now. The Stonebeings are the bones of the Earth Mother and they are your bones, too. They help you to feel safe and loved in your body now.

Electrical Body Alignment: We link you with your Spiritfamilies.

Affirmation of Support: *"I am unconditionally loved and I unconditionally love, now."*

Tools for Manifestation

Wear me quietly.
Listen more than you talk.
Everything and every being that appears on your path is a guide.
What are they saying?
If you don't know,
or don't remember,
put me on your heart.
Sigh into the Stonebeings.
Breathe into them all your yearning and freedom.
Your heart translates all.

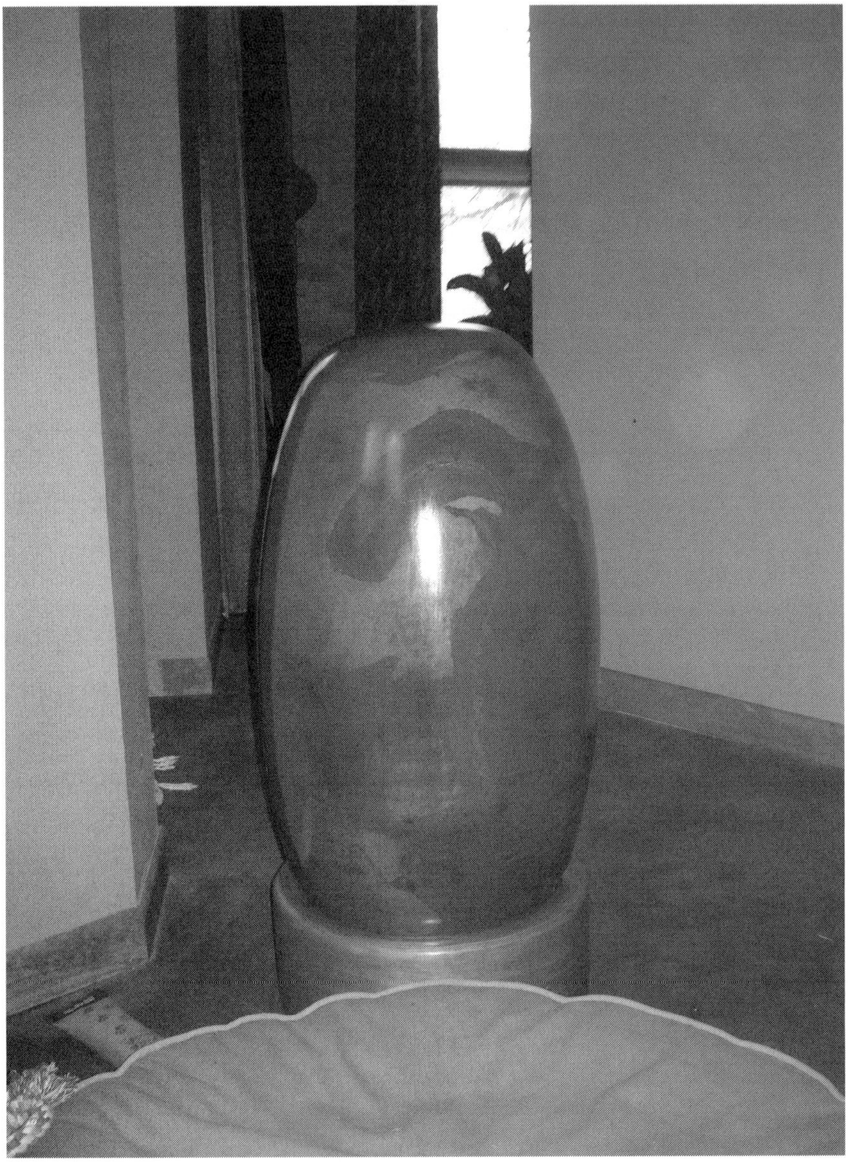

This 500 pound, approximately 4 foot tall Lingam lives in a sacred geometry, live home and business, built specifically to hold the space for freedom, immortality and invisibility and personal life regeneration.

Whisperings......

Feel it.

Feel the pulsating beneath your feet.

If you don't remember it, put your bare toes on the Earth Mother.

Ask them to find it.

Find it...

Find it...

Find it now...

and now.

Follow it like a drum beat.

Permeate your being with it.

It is an eternal song of life

and it is between us

constantly in measure

and at once gorgeously, wildly, undefined by any limits.

Breathe it.

This is how we find each other.

When you listen to the hearts of the Stonebeings here

immerse yourself in our endless beat.

A JOURNEY to the CENTER of the CRYSTALLINE GRID

Be in a completely quiet space.

Be in a cave.

Or make one to be in.

Surround yourself in the release of silence and darkness. Let them clothe you so that all expectations will drift away and never have to be owned again.

Breathe gently.

Allow each breath complete consideration as an honored guest of your body. Let them travel wherever they will go. There is no pushing or pulling here. There is only allowing.

You cannot force your way upon the Grid. All you can do is cheerfully strip away the layers that you put between your feelings and it.

Your eyes are closed but relaxed. They are not forced shut. The lids simply join together, calmly.

This allows the eyes beneath to be alert, to spin in their knowingness, if and when they choose to do so.

Most of all, you are letting go of control.

As you exhale, your breath is called up from the roots of your cells and it flows out your pores, gracefully, constantly.

Now, if any control gets stuck leaving you, grasp your hands into fists. Feel all the fingers tightly touching each other. Let them bore into your palms. They will touch the chakras there.

Squeeze them and squeeze them, and then, when you are ready, let them and your breath pop open. Feel the life tingle back into your fingers, your palms.

Perhaps it is life you have not touched for a long time.

Place the backs of your hands gently on your body or at your side.

They are freer then they have ever been.

Let them nestle into you or into the Earth with no need to fulfill.

The palms will sink slightly.

The fingers will curl.

Your body will watch this opening back on itself,

peaceful, yet more alert than you know how to say.

Life is your being now. You no longer have to force your destiny.

The breaths will keep clearing and dusting away the remnants of shame and struggle.

Organs will grow anew.

Your lungs will regenerate as much as you will allow.

Either lay down or sit back, straight but relaxed, to encourage your body to fall into the Earth now, to slip inside the Mother that you have always wanted to embrace.

If you are afraid, just let the weight of you go away.

Hold nothing.

Your posture now will let everything within you renew.

Focus upon that when the fears try to distract you and they will. Do not think that they journey has gone wrong or that you are a bad person.

Whenever a being of separation enters true union, everything that they truly are is now free to be present with them. You are used to seeing your strengths and your ease. You shape your personality to stand so that you can view these.

When you let go into All-That-Is, when you release into the Grid as you are doing right now, the lights and the shadows will come into play and every color in between will show itself.

Courage simply means allowing yourself to see yourself.

With each breath, we are deeper in the Earth Mother where it is safer than you knew how to imagine.

Nothing can harm you.

The Earth is your guardian and the source of all life that you drink in here.

So, truly breathe now.

Breathe not just air, but all of the Elementals from all parts of your being.

Breathe in the cool dark as it renews you.

Breathe with eyes and hair and your womb.

Let your womb unfold into hers where there are Crystals and rivers and dreams.

Open your inner eye completely now.

It is as light or as dark as you need, to focus upon anything.

While your body is given to the Earth and unmoving, let your Spirit body now arise, unlimited, unashamed.

Let it walk inside the Earth.

We are in the cave with very long Crystals growing from the ground to the inner sky.

They hum with the vibration of all life.

We reach out and place Spirit hands upon them and stroke them.

Instead of feeling sharp and heavy, they yield to the lightest touch.

They move.

They bend with ease.

They create Air that we breathe like an aroma.

It fills us with such lightness that it is as if we explode, but we cannot, for we are already everywhere at once.

Sit before the clusters of Crystals.

Match heartbeats.

When you are ready, reach into your root.

Find the intent that you traveled here.

With your own heart, with your own words, freely give your intent to these Crystalline Guides.

Ask them to show you the Crystalline Grid.

Ask with no attachment.

Ask with full honoring of all that you are, even the darkest shadow,

with utter respect for your journey and your willingness,

with the clarity of all Crystals.

For the pure generosity of the Earth Mother is our model in life for all things.

After you ask, be still.

Be the Center Stillness.

Just be and breathe.

Everyone who journeys to the Center of the Earth, to the Crystalline Grid, will meet some kind of Guide.

In our journey together, now, we have just met an enormous Crystalline cluster in an Earth cave of great feeling.

You will not always remember the Guides.

Today you will.

Because I point them out to you.

They are here for whatever you need.

You cannot truly touch the Grid if you are still focused on lack and are allied with pain.

The Guides will hold your hands so that you can feel warm enough to let go of what you no longer need.

They will automatically inspire peace and calm, even if you are excited, even if you are afraid.

They will not take away your emotions.

They will not change anything of you or from you.

They will simply answer every question, every need, with calm.

You will be surrounded by so much calmness that it will be simpler to let go of your attachments than you ever knew it could be.

Thank the Guides.

Today they are an enormous cluster of Crystals growing in all directions, reaching to every being who is right now taking this journey.

They will appear to each of us in whatever form we will need.

When you remember this, you do not even have to be startled by how quickly and often they transform.

Inside the Earth Mother, all are shapeshifters.

Now breathe more deeply without willing it.

Just accept this new sweeter Air in more abundance than you have ever known before.

That is your fuel.

That is your focus.

The Guides have swept away whatever we no longer needed and were utterly free to cast aside.

They will take the worn out shadows, feed them Crystal prana and they themselves can become Guides now in the Earth Mother.

We are free.

We are standing in the center of the Crystalline Grid.

Now, open all your senses like a morning flower, wide and beautiful and utterly sensitive to everything.

We stand in the frame of a cube.

It is completely clear yet it flashes every color periodically.

Every scent and sound and taste and touch finds you yet they all go immediately.

They have no need to stay for you are fulfilled instantly, and then, they move, twist and transmute.

The cube becomes a circle, a hoop of life.

It matches the circle of every horizon so you will remember the Grid, inside and out.

Within the Grid, you are home.

You are recognized as the brave adventurer you have always been.

You weep because you are utterly known here.

Everytime you fell, everytime you tried to control, is here recorded, echoing, in the Grid and in your cells.

But now you know that it is not the cause of pain.

That it is here because it is still lifeforce and life belongs to life and when all of it is greeted with acceptance,

as it is here,

it shapeshifts, it mutates into the dreams that you have yearned for lovingly.

Right now the Crystalline Grid itself continually moves, forms and adds forms, to be the Utopia that you came here to know.

It breeds octahedrons and tulips and triangles and rivers and gardens of Stones and Agates and Clusters.

Keep watching.

Whatever you feel is being mirrored in the Crystalline Grid before you,

every true whim, translates into form.

If it is too cool for you, it grows a Sun or two, and they follow your every movement until you are warmed with such creativity that you become the Grid as well.

Watching all things materialize and spontaneously manifest, you realize you are made of and from these cells.

You look down at your hands and they are caves and Guides.

You look at your feet and they are the roots of the mightiest mountains above.

When you shiver with the thrill, they quake.

Back and forth, you and the Grid, transform spontaneously with each wish that you offer.

It is as if, with a single feeling, a Magi touches a wand to you in the Grid, saying, "It is so. Your wish is alive."

I do not want to tell you everything that happens here because you are the wise one.

You are the shape that the Grid will shift to and if I speak too much, your dream will start to match what you believe must be. And beliefs are not needed here.

We live lifeforce and it lives us and it creates constantly.

So I will be silent for a little while as YOU bring every wish to the Grid.

Bring ALL your feelings.

Let them come home.

Keep breathing.

Beyond here be your dreams.................

When you are at peace

and have nothing else that you have brought with to shape,

to say,

to sculpt,

to set free,

touch your heart

and touch the Grid.

Now you can always remember they are the same.

They are different facets from the same Crystal.

Give thanks.

Give honoring for the journey.

Be free.

Go back up now through the Earth,

excited to match this Earth heart to the one in your body.

Keep breathing with infinite space and time.

Settle your Spirit into your body which is smooth from release and held in the embrace of the Earth Mother.

You can see that now.

You have not always known that this was so.

But your ignorance has never stopped the truth and it never will.

You have just filled yourself with unlimited knowingness.

Every question and answer has already been matched and you have been set free by their union.

You no longer have need even when you experience it and you will.

Touch your hands to your heart.

Breathe through them.

This is your Crystalline Grid.

It has always been this way.

As long as you walk the Earth, you will carry the Grid in your two-legged shape and in every step.

It will shape the Earth to your vision.

It is easy to travel the Grid.

Now all that remains is to free and clarify your visions.

Breathe that until you are at home here and everywhere else and then open ALL your eyes to see what you are creating.

Take as much time as you need here to activate your co-created Grids so they can more fully root and ground in this present time and space, here and now.

This Lingam stands outside the front entrance to the home mentioned on page 206, and is the Greeter and the Guardian. It welcomes all things in Acceptance.

Whisperings......

All around us
swirl
geometries of life.
Put out your hand
touch the simple dirt.
Uncountable grains of sand reach back and
grasp your fingers.
No more thinking.
Touch the sand.
Each grain pulses.
It holds the heartbeat of life, itself
and shares it with you.
Your body knows.
Your body winks and grins.
Your heart echoes the heartbeat of life
whenever you
touch something
whenever you reach in and out
to caress the pulse of
anything you touch.
Drink in life itself.
Your blood ebbs, flows, sighs with oceans.
Your bones stand tall with mountains.

Your breath blows with winds.
As within, so without.
All of life nods.
Do you?

Within you is the Earth. It is your body, it is your being.
All around you is the Earth. It is your body, it is your being.
It is all of us.
We are the Earth
cell by cell
wave onto wave
inhale merging exhale
onto forever.

Before we talk more in this way
listen.
Listen so deeply to your body that you
recognize
all its kind ways of talking with you—
the physical words that land upon your awareness
even before pain
before stiffness
before dis-ease.
Your body, your Earth, reaches out to your heart—
the translator of all that is, the meeting place of life
and whispers.

It whispers so sweetly
almost anything could seem to overpower it.
When you're truly, heartfully listening
you hear the precious parts
first
continually
right on to the last sigh of your body.

Yes.
Now you hear and listen
to every sigh
to every eye blink
on a brightly sunny day.
Your Earthbody flows,
Leaps,
Dances,
with the shifting sands of the Earth.
Sharpen your listening.
Always hear whatever you need to hear
to know when your blood rises too high,
when your bones crave warmth.
Each part of your body,
each cell,
each finger,
each muscle,
knows the perfect ever-shifting balance between them now.

Allow it.
Your back will straighten gracefully.
Your neck will unlock.
Your eyes will see into time and space and beyond...
If you allow the flow
as you hear it,
as you feel it,
as you touch it,
you are the flow of life itself.
Be the Earth, itself.
It will dance you
like the song of love
you are.

Now, while you are ever listening to your
own Earth body
listen more (read on)
to the Earth Mother,
to her rivers,
to her spine,
to her breaths,
to her Crystalline Grid bones.
They have been whispering all along
so that you can move delightedly
with the flow of life,
itself.

Re-definition of Terms

In listening and learning with our Spirits, certain words form the foundation of the wisdom that is given us. They are repeated constantly, so that we can truly feel the **vibrations** *in the words—not just their literal definitions—and catalyze great change within us with those vibrations.*

We share both the meanings and the energies of some of those key words now. Remember, the definitions might be incidental (except that they may catalyze even more feelings); the vibrations of the words as they are used will resonate within your being so you can find new choices and new life, as you wish. Repeat them often, for you may change every time you hear them and then receive new gifts. Happy adventuring~

ACCEPTANCE— is the **practice** of unconditional love, because unconditional love just is.

DETACHMENT— is the constant practice of freedom, even when parts of your being are not free. You see, as unconditional love, you also know and live with conditional love; it is simply accepted, not separated. Detachment is the practice that accepts the un-free parts of life and still accepts and practices freedom.

ELEMENTALS— are the Devic Spirits of the Elements that comprise all matter upon the Earth: Earth/Fire/Water/Air/Ethers. Each element represents certain emotional and spiritual qualities besides the physical ones, especially Ethers which is the Spirit and consciousness in all things and beings. When you align with the Elementals, you align with the core of life and creativity.

FREEDOM— is the manifestation of acceptance. It is the beingness in every doing. It is the uncontainable in each structure. It offers equal respect to all.

IMMORTALITY— is the manifestation of your freedom and invisibility. Because all of these things are faces of unconditional love, immortality is the "more" that is given back to you for your commitment and your practices—not as a condition—but simply for the creation of it.

INVISIBILITY— is the practice of freedom. It is the commitment in the face of all circumstances to be free. It invites detachment. It is magic. It allows you the fuel to move between the worlds. Think of it as a magician's cloak that only you can perceive. It carries you seamlessly into anything.

SEPARATION— is what every human experiences by being born. We are truly divine beings here to have a human experience. While in these bodies, we will forget for a little while that we are also Spirits who will always be connected to everything, even though we wear bodies that apparently are separate from everything. It takes a lot of time and energy to learn separation and then it requires great focus to practice it as a lifestyle and as a consensual reality. It is the source of our pain, struggle, fear and learning.

We experience separation so that one day we will remember that we are, in fact, connected to everything. Then we will offer our unconditional life to union AND to separation, so that nothing in life is unaccepted and unloved.

SUPER HERO— is your special brand of genius. Each of us has learned through our schools and traditions to conform. The Super hero in us (which by the way is absolutely innate in everyone's being) stays alive, and creates ever more life, by being the unique divinity that Spirit has given us. If we don't offer those gifts to life, then no one else will. No one else can do and be us. So, as Super heroes, our mission is to be thoroughly ourselves and then share that open-heartedly with the world. In doing this, we become more and more empowered and even create new gifts to be and to share.

UNCONDITIONAL LOVE— is exponential lifeforce. It always gives more than it takes. Addiction/Attachment always takes more than it gives.

Afterwords

So here we are. We have traveled to the end of this book-adventure, together, and instead of just seeing the end, we find the dawn coming up surer and stronger than ever before. With all our hearts and sighs, we thank you for this gorgeous journey together.

With this book, we have just fed you a slice of our life. We listen to our Spirits and any respectful Stonebeings and Naturebeings who have gifts they have asked to share with us, now. To be able to also pass that on to our two-legged friends, almost takes away all our words and just leaves tears. Thank you. We know that it is a little different to be listening so much to other, non-human children of the Earth. Yet, we are all family and if we truly live that now, everything will change for all of us, most especially we two-leggeds. For Tohmas and I, that is the dream that dawns, powerfully and truly, before us every moment, every sigh, every heart-opening, every thought, and every act.

So join us further, now, if you will. This is the most wide-open life adventure invitation we can offer to your wondrous heart right now. What you have felt here, already, is one facet of an exquisite, ever-evolving crystal of listening. In our life-adventure, we have listened with: the Earth Mother; Gandarvas, the land that we live with/on; human babies in utero; people in comas; dogs, cats, parrots, snakes that live with humans; storms; ourselves at other ages; friends and family who have passed on to their next adventure, and so much more.

Our Spiritfamilies have directly asked us to share all of this, with you, through the following services and tools. They have worked with us in all of these things for years and years, and now it is time to share them in this Earth evolution that is touching us all so deeply. They will support you; that is our experience and we share that, with our hearts, now:

Where to Get the Most Timely Updates

Call or email us. Check our websites at **www.ahhhmuse.com** and **www.abundanceofahhhmuse.com** We put our lives, our stories and pictures there for all the world to see. Welcome! We are constantly co-creating with our Spirits as they spur us onto ever greater miracles to keep up with the second-to-second changing vibration of the Earth Mother and her beings!! So of course the poor (but valiant) web sites don't quite keep up with us. No matter. If you don't immediately see what you need there, just call (575-534-0410); we'll find what you need. Email anytime (ahhhmuse@juno.com). We are here; this is why we are on the Earth. You're reading this now to receive this invitation from our hearts. It is here for you. Accept it.

Our Services

Personal Listenings

We offer listening consultations in as many forms as there are needs.

Private listenings/readings— Whenever you need to get an unconditionally accepting perspective on your story, we're here. We'll listen to your Spiritfamilies and see what they have been just waiting to offer you on your amazing path. We are all evolving as quickly and as powerfully as we can. Why not be utterly supported in that? A different perspective— a word from Spirit—can completely revive you and find you unlimited options from which to manifest new life. We know from our own experience that hearing from our Spirits guides us, but mostly, it so helps us not to feel alone when we are struggling and hurt. Sometimes, just that feeling changes everything instantly, even when you thought that was impossible.

Astrology listenings/readings— Astrology is a gorgeous language that witnesses how everything in the heavens and on the earth flows in perfect, divine cycles with each other. The same cycles flow within you—the way the phases of the Moon interweave with the ocean's tides and the blood in our bodies. Everything utterly interconnects. Instead of fighting what is naturally happening (even subconsciously), you can go with it and respectfully use it to be whatever you truly choose in the most harmonious, respectful way possible. I (Marilyn) will listen to your chart and let it unfold its story in exactly the ways you most need to hear, now. Here are some of the finest ways I have been able to utilize and share astrology (and I'm OPEN to wherever your respectful heart leads):

New businesses
New babies
Relationship & family support
Manifesting your dreams
Caring for your body
Focusing on and expanding your talents
Finding times that support specific activities

Personal Story

Some years ago, Spirit asked me to find a Stone that included Black Tourmaline and Quartz and I went out with Tohmas to find such a stone, not knowing that I would hit on an amazing combination of stones—Black Tourmaline, Quartz, Mica and Feldspar, all in one 222 lb package.

This patient stone has been at the entrance of my triple domed home for some years now providing protection and love. One day, when I feared that I had lost most of my money, I went to my "guardian stone", crying, "What am I going to do? What am I going to dooooo?" A very clear message came to me: "Go To The Studio!" I did as I was asked, and began a sculpture which brought into light my fears of aging and brought me instant tranquility as well.

I will never forget that day because I realized then that all I have to do is "ask," and the answers come. Laying my hands on my "guardian stone," and focusing on its beingness, I feel soothed, loved, grounded and at peace.

I am grateful.

~Ursela

Sacred Space Consultations

If you want to build anything: an office, a home, a healing center, or any kind of structure, there is a Spirit that already lives with that form, even before it has completely birthed on the Earth. We will listen to it and help you to co-create it in the most glorious, harmonious way possible.

If you want to build a home that will house your Spirit and regenerate your body, we have done them (hands-on). We begin by listening to the Earth Mother to see where it wishes to welcome you and what kind of design will bring sacredness to your own body-spirit integration while simultaneously honoring all the plants, animals and minerals already living there.

New Body-Spirit Scans and Listenings

Elemental Birth Imprints— At the exact moment of your birth, the Elementals (the Devic Spirits of the Elements that comprise all matter upon the Earth: Fire; Earth; Air; Water; Ethers, and Ethers are the Spirit-that-Moves-in-all-Things) imprint your body with a sole Element or more likely, a combination of Elements that will speak of your core tendencies and learnings from a very basic, superbly helpful view. For instance, if you were born with a Fire and Water Elemental Birth Imprint, you will discover that emotions lead you in almost everything. If you accept this, it will be your gift to share; if you reject it, it can rule your life with unintended, constant, unproductive dramas.

You can learn how your imprint manifests in your life and how you can change and grow with it very effectively, and how it will combine with others' imprints. And if you find that helpful, ask us about your Conceptional Elemental Imprint~

Crystal Body Graphs— It is our joy to connect with the Earth Spirits AND also with kind and wise Starbeings who give us a bigger perspective than we can conceive of while on the Earth. We love listening with Pleiadeans, such as the Crystal Builder, who talks about refining technologies and anything that we build here, including our bodies. With your permission, we can pass on how your emotions, thoughts and patterns are continually creating your body, your health

Personal Story

I have obtained many wondrous items from Ahhhmuse over the past year, and one year does not accurately reflect a relationship and deep connection which I feel certain encompasses many lifetimes since spirit reunited us in this time and place. If I were to tell you about each precious gift I have been fortunate enough to obtain, my flow of words would certainly go on and on. But, I find there is no need to speak of each separately because in describing one, I find that the same words truly apply to all, each and every one.

So, whether I am talking about the Magi, the Deva's Gift Crystal Singing Bowl, the Vibrational Jewelry, the many stonebeings, or the stonessences, I can simply, honestly and gladly say they are all divine gifts of immense power, wisdom and love. Each has been a mentor, a parent, friend or Beloved to me. However, I would not be saying all that must be said if I did not also share the love, appreciation, gratitude and deep respect I have for the two beautiful people who serve

(con't on next page)

and your life. This wisdom is all-encompassing, very direct, and very immediate.

Body Alignment Scans— If you like, we can spontaneously scan your body and let you know how it is regenerating itself. Often times, your body will let us know the specific foods; herbs; movements; sounds; rituals, etc., that will spontaneously revitalize it. We have scanned our bodies for a very long time and it is our most practical way to institute immediate change and to support its long term integration into our life.

Relating to the Animal/Mineral/Plant Kingdoms— Everybody has totems in the kingdoms of life on the Earth that speak to them directly and profoundly, in ways that nothing else can. It is our joy to translate those messages to you, as you wish. Or if you prefer, we can listen with the animals that live with you to help you learn and grow together more gloriously all the time.

Spiritcoaching and the Freedom Intent

For a long time, our Spiritfamilies have talked with us every day of how the Earth Mother (and we) are evolving and how we can co-create our realities, with respectful, immediate rituals. They tell us that it is time for us to share that with any two-leggeds who are willing to learn whatever their Spirits want to co-create with them. Once you have stated your intent then our Spirits let us know if it is respectful and honoring for us to work together at this time. If it is, then they will offer us a plan where we will work together regularly in specific rituals for a specified time. Those parameters are designed completely for you and for your current, unique needs. Through the Spiritcoaching, we become the constant, unconditional support crew in your loving co-creations with your Spirit.

Freedom Intent— Our Spirit Grandmother designed this intensive, which usually manifests as a kind of vision quest where together we will focus ONLY on your connection to Spirit, without the noise, distractions or addictions of the two-legged world.

The Freedom Intent (and we have lived many) invites you fully to do nothing but listen with and co-create with your Spirit, so you can go more deeply into your spiritual journey than ever before. We will listen

as the Keepers, Guardians, and Wisdom Teachers, who ensure that we always, and in all ways, receive that which is for our highest good, while also honoring and listening for whatever each beautifully alive item, being and/or gift wishes to come and be with us. And, they do it all with the utmost love and respect, accompanied by a fantastic sense of humor.

Dearest Marilyn and Tohmas, I love each of you and the service you provide to Spirit, the Earth and all of her many inhabitants.

I love you both.

~Aranyah

and be with you constantly, for whatever timeframe your Spirit asks of you and usually it is two weeks.

Workshops

We love to travel and offer as many different workshops as you could possibly like: What would truly thrill you?

Some of our offerings are: Listening with Stones; Co-Creating Sacred Space; Rituals of Manifestation; Aligning with the Elementals. We continually update these workshops with spiritpractices to help us live, thrive and evolve with the Earth Mother and her constantly changing vibration.

Stone Listening for You and Your Business

Our Spirits asked us to co-create AhhhMuse (our business) as a sacred vehicle for sharing their words and ways and tools to give the most support possible to evolving humans: Books; The Rituals of Manifestation Deck; Stonessences; Vibrational Jewelry; The Act of Power Wands; Lifenhancers; CD's; the Deva's Gift Crystal Singing Bowls. Please come visit our website at **www.ahhhmuse.com** to see that and much more.

In our work, we also attract very unique Stonebeings who come to live with us for a while to feel the utter respect we offer them. We listen to them, we live with them and we manifest with them, just as they wish. From there, they travel to other people who will then work with them in their own unique ways.

As you wish, we listen to Stonebeings to come to you or your business. For many years now, the vast majority of Stonebeings we have sold have been gone to people and businesses, sight unseen. They trusted in the energy of the Stonebeings speaking to them and unexpected miracles have sprung from this every time.

Here are our hearts. Here are the offerings of our Spirits. Thank you for listening. We share them with you because it supports us and our life, but most of all because our Spirits have asked to be bridges between willing humans and all other loving beings upon the Earth. Our bodies translate all those languages and help that magic land in human lives in a way that they can easily understand for themselves. All of this springs from the deepest part of our beings and our sacred practices of life and they are manifest upon the Earth for all to see and to share as they wish. Thank you always and in all ways.

Sacred Witnessing

Personal Story

Dear Mrs.Twintreess,

Namaste

How are you and Mr Twintreess? If I have disturbed you I am very sorry.

Today I started reading "Stones Alive!" and its wonder full! First of all I opened the book to know something about Rubys but when I started reading the first page, I could not stop reading.

Its so deep, actually far beyond my understanding but I tried to absorb the depth of wisdom hidden in every line. The "quote," "Affirmation of Support," & "Stone Story," are very deep. I had to pause between every sentence to understand what it was trying to say. I touched surface of some understanding but felt that I could think for hours and never totally figure out its total meaning. I have only finished reading 40 pages.

If you have time, can you explain the difference between Soul and Spirit, or are they same? Can Stones store human memories?

I really like "the Stone Story" (but wish they were in simpler language). Well I have realized that great minds never use simple words.

I also very much want to read each book of Harry Potter but presently they are under locks and keys and under watchfull eyes of my mother because she thinks if I read Harry Potter so much I may degrade my performance at school.

With regards

Rishi C.

(Age 16, Katmandu, Nepal)

Personal Story

I was looking for a Black Phantom Quartz and because of the characteristics of this crystal it felt like I should get it (not-knowing that they are a rare crystal). I thought Marilyn could help me in finding one. She and Tohmas were going to the Tucson Gem Show and said that maybe they could find one there. But after a few weeks of waiting, still no find. I kind of forgot about it for awhile until Marilyn wrote me and said that she hadn't forgotten and was still looking. A couple more weeks went by and I didn't hear from her. On one of those nights I had a dream that I got the Black Phantom, it was being handed to me and I said, "This is it! This is the Crystal!" It was clear with rings of black in it, and it felt very potent and happy. The very next day Marilyn wrote saying they found some crystals and had pictures of them. When I was looking through the pictures one popped out and it felt like deja' vu. It was a Tibetan Crystal with Black Phantom rings in it, exactly the same crystal that was in my dream the night before!!

With love and service

~Ben H.

Personal Story

Potential Quartz...is about...support in
exuding one's potential...
it's a beautiful stone...even though one might not
initially think so....
a natural citrine covered in a veil of white sugar
crystals...
hence the potential...inside...

in 2007 we requested one such stone from Ahhhmuse....
coming from brazil, it felt as though it was hand
selected by tohmas....
500 lbs worth!
delivered to our new home in Sedona...
and masterfully placed on top of a pine tree
trunk!....8 feet tall...

the energy was immediately felt ...an enormous
presence of peace and grounding...
we really...had no idea what else was in store until we
began taking pictures of the kitchen dome...and
noticed that huge orbs were emanating from the
cluster!

Personal Story

I have a cool story about Selenite. On the day before the well drillers were scheduled to come and drill the well here at my new home, I was meeting Marilyn in town. When we finished our business, she invited me to close my eyes and put out my hands, and she put a heavy stone with a strong vertical grain into them. "What do you feel?"she asked. Once I got past my internal programming of, "I don't know anything about crystals," I could listen, and what I felt was bubbles, so I just said it was bubbly. She asked me to open my eyes, and told me it was Selenite, and how it forms in water.

This connected immediately for me with the well-drilling, so I excitedly took it home with me. In the area where I live, the surrounding wells are 500– 600 feet deep, and not terribly productive, and in the larger area here, there are many up to 1,000 feet or more. Water is an issue on this land.

That night I put the Selenite next to my pillow and asked for its help as I stated my Intent for

(con't on next page)

what a delight to have the presence of sprites...delicious company!

we are so grateful to Ahhhmuse for their infinite connection to the crystal kingdom...and their knowing of "Stones Alive!"....

~Alice and Eileen

us to find abundant, life-giving water quickly and easily the next day.

In the morning, I wanted to keep the Selenite with me, so I brought it and introduced it to the drillers as our support in this process. I anticipated they'd think I was crazy, but in that moment that wasn't as important to me as staying aligned with the stone, and it was asking to be acknowledged in this way.

So they drilled, and water started spitting out at 25 feet, and just kept getting stronger as they went deeper. The drillers were dumbfounded to find so much water so close to the surface, and I have been blessed with abundant delicious water from this Source ever since.

I thank Marilyn's and my listening and the Selenite's support for this amazing gift.

~Lynn A.

Personal Story

Dear Mrs Twintreess,

Namaste. I am very fine, thank you. I have finished reading the book, Stones Alive! and am shocked about my ignorance towards the magic that was so close to me. Yes, yes, yes, I would really like my thoughts to be in your book. But its quite scary too. It is a matter of great honor for me to be in book so deep and quite enlightening (if we could do as Stonebeings asks us). But I do not at all want it to happen if Stonebeings do not want me to be in their book. I have finished the book but will read again from my heart not from my mind (like you said). I really like this book because it taught me about magic that was different.

From my thoughts, I only believed in "Harry Potter" magic. I found this book very educational. I liked some points very much that I copied them in my diary!

Like:

- *Every thing that we are is love.*
- *We have to live not just survive.*
- *New ideas might be the only real fear we find in life.*
  Nothing goes with me but my choice to go there, etc, etc, etc.

There are many more. I wish that I could apply these points in my life, but I do not think that I am that focused or determined to do so.

Is pearl also a stonebeing? I could not find it in the book or was I too careless while reading to find it? If I can give you and Mr. Twintreess an advice? I would like you allow me to say a tiny thing. I think the book would be more informative if there were pictures of those stonebeing(crystal). It would make us (peoples who are the beginners like me, who are not familiar with the vast universe of stones) know how they look, what are their physical structure.

I was amazed by Stone Combination Section, the way you combine different minerals to give us power to change our self and our nature.

I want to say one thing I always wanted to tell you both. That for me, you look like a kind angel and Mr Twintreess looks like a wise lord. (Quite silly of me though).

With regards,

~Rishi C.

Personal Story

My husband Dave had seen some Elestial Smokey Quartz crystals at the Springfield Gem Show. He really wanted one, but none of the ones there seemed to be the one for him. He asked me if the Twintreess had things like the ones we had looked at. I told him that I bet they did and that if they didn't they could find one for him.

We asked Tohmas to go shopping for us at the Tucson Gem Show and had given him a description of what Dave was looking for. I was a bit surprised at the confidence Dave had in Tohmas, considering the only contact he had with them was through seeing the few wonderful pieces I had gotten over the past couple of years. I was also rather surprised at the generous budget Dave gave Tohmas so easily. Dave is a bargain hunter and a picky shopper to say the least. However, he seemed to have no trouble handing the wheel over to Tohmas! When the universe goes to work with the Twintreess as agents, watch out! Amazing things happen!

A few weeks later the package arrived. I struggled to heave it into the house. It was a big one! In it, we were told, were two Smokey Elestials Tohmas had purchased for us. I was curious and eager to get the box open. The first of the two was a huge, glittering Smokey Elestial that must have weighed 20 lbs! It was stunning! I just sat and stared at it and tried to remember to breathe! It is a true blessing to have it in our home and our lives. BUT THE SECOND piece! I was not prepared. I unwrapped it from the paper and immediately felt a stunning presence. Never before, although I have many wonderful pieces, had I seen one like this, not in a museum, collection, not anywhere. I felt as though I had come into the presence of a sacred being of incredible stillness, holiness and peace. What it is about how these thing work I do not know, nor can I really explain.

A dear friend of ours, upon meeting this incredible Stone Being, named "him" Brownie. When ever we go for a visit, which always involves the sharing of Stones and Stone healing, the door opens for us. "Did you bring Brownie?" she asks through the crack in the door opening. We sometimes wondered if we were going to be turned away if perhaps Brownie was not in the bag at our side! For at least 6 months Brownie was with us whereever we went (almost!). Some people have a poodle in a pocketbook. We have a 10 pound Smokey Elestial Malawi crystal. Now Brownie lies beside our bed, and participates in many healing sessions with us at home and away.

Don't let the name fool you. Although Brownie is as comforting and rich as the dessert he is named after, we know he is so much more than that!

PS. This year, our dear friend sent Tohmas out shopping again at Tucson. Now she has her own, unique Malawi too! We call him "Brownie 2". Really. He is as special, although totally unique in himself, as our own special Brownie. Thank you Tohmas and Marilyn!

~Liz and Dave C.

Index